Impact Listening

Kenton Harsch

Kate Wolfe-Quintero

Series Editor
Michael Rost

3

PEARSON
Longman

Published by
Pearson Longman Asia ELT
20/F Cornwall House
Taikoo Place
979 King's Road
Quarry Bay
Hong Kong

The publisher's policy is to use **paper manufactured from sustainable forests**

fax: +852 2856 9578
email: pearsonlongman@pearsoned.com.hk
www.longman.com

and Associated Companies throughout the world.

This book was developed for Longman Asia ELT by Lateral Communications Limited.

First edition 2001
This edition 2007 (reprinted twice)

Produced by Pearson Education Asia Limited, Hong Kong
SWTC/03

PROJECT DIRECTOR, SERIES EDITOR: Michael Rost
PROJECT COORDINATOR: Keiko Kimura
PROJECT EDITOR: Aaron Zachmeier
ART DIRECTOR: Inka Mulia
TEXTBOOK DESIGN: Inka Mulia
PRODUCTION COORDINATOR: Rachel Wilson
ILLUSTRATIONS: Ben Shanon, Violet Lemay
PHOTOGRAPHS: Bananastock, Blue Moon, Brand X Pictures, Dynamic Graphics, Iconotect, i dream stock, Image Source, Image Zoo, Inmagine, MIXA, Photodisc, Pixtal, Rubberball, Stockbyte, Tong Ro Image Photographers

AUDIO ENGINEER: Glenn Davidson
MUSIC: Music Bakery
TEST CONSULTANTS: Gary Buck, Natalie Chen
WEBSITE COORDINATOR: Keiko Kimura

IMPACT LISTENING 1

SB + CD	ISBN-13: 978-962-00-5801-1	ISBN-10: 962-00-5801-1
TM + Test CDs	ISBN-13: 978-962-00-5804-2	ISBN-10: 962-00-5804-6
Class CDs	ISBN-13: 978-962-00-5807-3	ISBN-10: 962-00-5807-0

IMPACT LISTENING 2

SB + CD	ISBN-13: 978-962-00-5802-8	ISBN-10: 962-00-5802-X
TM + Test CDs	ISBN-13: 978-962-00-5805-9	ISBN-10: 962-00-5805-4
Class CDs	ISBN-13: 978-962-00-5808-0	ISBN-10: 962-00-5808-9

IMPACT LISTENING 3

SB + CD	ISBN-13: 978-962-00-5803-5	ISBN-10: 962-00-5803-8
TM + Test CDs	ISBN-13: 978-962-00-5806-6	ISBN-10: 962-00-5806-2
Class CDs	ISBN-13: 978-962-00-5809-7	ISBN-10: 962-00-5809-7

Acknowledgements

The authors and editors would like to thank the many teachers and students who have used the *Impact Listening* series for their feedback. We also wish to thank the following people who contributed ideas, resources, stories, reviews and other feedback that helped us in the development of the second edition of the *Impact Listening* series:

Glenn Agius	Selana Allen	Kayra Arias
Sara Barrack	E. Biddlecombe	Jennifer Bixby
Eric Black	Erin Boorse	Christina Boyd
Rob Brezny	Jennie Brick	Karen Carrier
Richard Carter	Andrea Carvalho	Lydia Chen
Yen-yen Chen	Feodor Chin	Jeniffer Cowitz
Terry Cox	Kevin Davey	Payton Davis
Sandy Eriksen	Christine Feng	Andrew Finch
Masayoshi Fukui	Greg Gamaza	Mark Girimonte
Ann Gleason	Greg Gomina	Allison Gray
Marvin Greene	Scott Grinthal	Naomi Hagura
William Hayes	Patrick Heller	James Hobbs
Jessie Huang	Sarah Hunt	Caroline Hwang
Jason Jeffries	Wonchol Jung	Alex Kahn
An-Ran Kim	Ju Sook Kim	Akiko Kimura
Barbara Kucer	Norm Lambert	Elizabeth Lange
Ruth Larimer	Tae Lee	Wayne Lee
Jason Lewis	Li-chun Lu	Rami Margron
Amy McCormick	Alexander Murphy	Amy Murphy
Andre Nagel	Dalia Nassar	Petra Nemcova
Tim Odne	Jamie Olsen	Joy Osmanski
John Park	Jeremy Parsons	Jackie Pels
Jessica Raaum	Stacey Reeve	Kerry Rose
Amy Rubinate	Alicia Rydman	Elly Schottman
Jerome Schwab	Ellen Schwartz	Sam Shih
Sherry Shinn	Josh Snyder	Jim Swan
Craig Sweet	Donna Tatsuki	Steven Thomas
Nicke Toree	Steven Trost	Aurelie Vacheresse
Joanna Vaughn	Yao-yao Wei	Paul Weisser
J. J. White	Julie Winter	Johnny Wong
Carolyn Wu	Cesar Zepeda	

We also wish to thank our colleagues at Pearson Longman for their guidance and support during the development of the second edition of the series. In particular, we'd like to acknowledge (Hong Kong) Roy Gilbert, Christienne Blodget, Rachel Wilson, Tom Sweeney, Michael Chan, Eric Vogt, Vessela Gasper; (Japan) Shinsuke Ohno, Minoru Ikari, Jonah Glick, Takashi Hata, Yuji Toshinaga, Steve King, Masaharu Nakata, Donn Ogawa, Yuko Tomimasu, Mari Hirukawa, Hiroko Nagashima, Megumi Takemura, Alastair Lamond, Michiyo Mitamura, Ken Sasaki, Takeshi Kamimura, Meiko Naruse, Tomoko Ayuse, Kenji Sakai, Reiko Murota, Mayumi Abe, Minako Uta, Masako Yanagawa, Ayako Tomekawa, Katherine Mackay, Keiko Sugiyama; (Korea) Yong Jin Oh, Chong Dae Chung, Jan Totty, Rilla Roessel, Katherine Ji, Hyuk Jin Kwon, Tae Youp Kim, Sang Ho Bae, Moon Jeong Lim; (Taiwan) Golden Hong, Louis Lin, Constance Mo, Vivian Wang, Sherrie Lin, Christine Huang, Joseph Chan, David Ger; (Thailand) Narerat Ancharepirat, Chris Allen, Unchalee Boonrakvanich, Udom Sathawara, Sura Suksingh;

Special thanks to Jason Lewis, Expedition 360, Maw-Maw's Cajun Kitchen, the rock band Pink, Tech Trek, Maxima Corporation Japan Ltd., Earthfoot Ecotours, Hardscratch Press, $RealMoney$ Enterprises®, Petra Nemcova and Warner Books for permission to use an extract from *Love Always, Petra* © 2005 Warner Books.

Introduction

The *Impact Listening* series is an innovative set of learning materials that helps students develop listening skills for social, academic and business purposes.

The series has three levels:
Impact Listening 1 (for beginning level students)
Impact Listening 2 (for high-beginning and low-intermediate students)
Impact Listening 3 (for intermediate and high-intermediate students)

Impact Listening makes listening an active and enjoyable experience for students. While featuring an abundance of natural listening input and a variety of creative activities, *Impact Listening* leads students to become successful listeners through an effective **4-step process**:

Step 1: Build word-based listening skills	Warm Up

To be successful listeners, we have to hear words and phrases accurately. With the **Warm Up**, each unit begins by helping students understand high-frequency words and phrases. As students become confident in their ability to "catch" common words and phrases, they increase their capacity for listening to longer stretches of language.

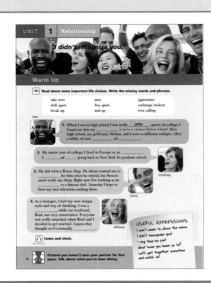

This section introduces common words and phrases related to the unit theme. With its interactive format, **Warm Up** gets all students involved at the outset of the lesson.

Step 2: Develop focusing strategies	Listening Task

It is important to have a purpose when we listen. Setting a purpose allows the students to become active listeners. In **Listening Task**, students are given a variety of tasks to focus their attention. A short follow-up speaking activity allows students to express their own ideas. They develop active listening strategies: **Prepare**, **Guess**, and **Focus**.

The section is a set of **two linked tasks** based on short natural listening extracts. The **First Listening** task focuses on understanding the gist, while the **Second Listening** task focuses on details. Vivid illustrations and photographs help students focus on meaning.

Step 3:
Practice idea-based strategies

Everyone experiences difficulties when listening to a second language. While they work on building effective word-based (bottom-up) listening skills, it is also important that students practice idea-based (top-down) listening strategies. In **Real World Listening**, students work on key listening strategies: **Ask**, **Respond**, and **Review**.

Real World Listening

Based on natural, extended conversations, monologues, and stories, this section helps students develop active listening strategies: predicting, inferring, clarifying, making judgments and responding to the ideas in the extract.

Step 4:
Integrate what you have learned

Connecting to the topic is a vital part of becoming a better listener. Throughout each unit, students are given the opportunity to develop curiosity, activate their knowledge, and express their ideas and opinions. **Interaction Link** helps students link listening and speaking.

Interaction Link

Interaction Link is a lively interactive speaking and listening task. Students have the opportunity to review what they have learned in the unit and use interactive tasks to produce real communication.

Impact Listening also includes

Self-Study pages

For use with the Self-Study CD (included in the back of every Student Book), the Self-Study page provides new tasks for the Real World Listening extract, to allow students to review at home. (Answer Key is provided.)

Teacher's Manual

Teachers are encouraged to utilize the *Impact Listening* Teacher's Manual. This manual contains teacher procedures, insightful language and culture notes, full scripts, answer keys, and expansion activities. The Teacher's Manual also includes a Test Master CD-ROM and instructions for creating and

Website

Teachers and students are welcome to use the *Impact Listening* series website for additional ideas and resources.
www.impactseries.com/listening

To the Student

Impact Listening will help you use listening strategies. Listening strategies are ways of thinking actively as you listen. Here are the main strategies you will practice in this course:

Prepare

- Preparing helps you listen better.
- Before you listen, look at the illustrations and photographs. Think about the ideas.
- Look over the vocabulary words.
- Try to predict what the speakers will say.

Ask

- Good listeners ask a lot of questions.
- While you listen, think of questions: What do you want to know?

Become an Active Listener

Guess

- Guessing can make you a more successful listener.
- Make your best guess at the parts you don't understand.

Respond

- Responding is part of listening!
- While you listen, pay attention to the speaker's ideas and intentions.
- After you listen, respond to the ideas: What do you think?

Focus

- Focus = Listen with a purpose.
- Before you listen, look at the listening task or questions.
- While you listen, focus on the task and questions. Listen for key words.
- If there are some words you don't understand, that's OK. Keep listening.

Review

- Reviewing builds your "listening memory."
- After you listen, think about the meaning of what the speakers have said.
- Try to say the meaning in your own words.

Contents

Contents

"*I didn't recognize you.*"

Warm Up

 Read about some important life choices. Write the missing words and phrases.

take over *перенимать*	into	apprentice
drift apart	free spirit	exchange student
break up	end up	true calling

Joe

1. When I was in high school, I was really ___into___ sports. In college I found out that my _____ is to be a science fiction writer! After high school, my girlfriend, Melissa, and I went to different colleges. After a while, we just _____ed _____.

2. My junior year of college I lived in Europe as an _____. I _____ed _____ going back to New York for graduate school.

Lindsay

3. My dad owns a flower shop. He always wanted me to _____ for him when he retired, but flowers really aren't my thing. Right now I'm working as an _____ to a famous chef. Someday I hope to have my own television cooking show.

Chris

4. As a teenager, I had my own unique style and way of thinking. I was a _____, while my boyfriend, Brad, was very conservative. Everyone was really surprised when Brad and I decided to get married. I guess they thought we'd eventually _____.

Allison

 Now listen and check.
CD 1, Track 2

 Pretend you haven't seen your partner for five years. Talk about what you've been doing.

USEFUL EXPRESSIONS
I can't seem to place the name.
I didn't recognize you!
Long time no see!
What have you been up to?
Let's get together sometime and catch up!

Look at the pictures. These people haven't seen each other in a long time. What are they talking about?

 First Listening: What has each person been doing? Check (✔) the true activities.

CD 1, Tracks 3–7

- ✔ traveling in Europe
- ✔ living in Boston
- ☐ studying European history

- ☑ apprenticing as a chef
- ☐ getting a business degree
- ☐ learning how to run a restaurant

- ☐ working as an accountant
- ☑ going to business school
- ☐ studying medicine

- ☐ becoming a judge
- ☐ working as a lawyer
- ☐ styling hair

 Second Listening: How does the other person react?

CD 1, Tracks 3–7

1.
- ✔ He isn't surprised that Jake lived abroad.
- ☐ He thinks Jake should stay in the U.S.

2.
- ☐ She didn't know Terry's family owned a restaurant.
- ☑ She wants to eat at Terry's restaurant.

3.
- ☐ He doesn't remember much about high school.
- ☐ He thinks Ken should have studied art.

4.
- ☐ She is surprised by Cindy's physical appearance.
- ☐ She doesn't think Cindy is a good lawyer.

PREPARE

Karen and Charisse haven't seen each other for many years.
One sentence about each woman is NOT true. Which do you think it is?

Karen

- ☐ moved to Hollywood.
- ☐ got a small part in a horror movie.
- ☐ is still in the movie business.
- ☐ is an actress.

Charisse

- ☐ married her high-school boyfriend Craig.
- ☐ is living in L.A.
- ☐ is working at an advertising company.
- ☐ just got a promotion.

🎧 **Now listen and check.**

CD 1, Tracks 8–9

GET THE MAIN IDEAS

🎧 Both women changed their plans in life. What did they want to do?
What did they end up doing?

CD 1,
Tracks 8–9

Karen wanted to ☐ be an actress.
  ☐ be a director.

She ended up ☐ as a waitress.
  ☐ as a makeup artist.

Charisse wanted to ☐ be a teacher.
  ☐ be a mother.

She ended up ☐ becoming an executive.
  ☐ becoming a professor.

RESPOND TO THE IDEAS

1. Who do you think changed the most, Karen or Charisse? Why?
2. Things happened in Karen's and Charisse's lives that they didn't expect. Tell a partner about something that you thought would happen in your life that didn't end up exactly as you expected.

TEN YEARS FROM NOW

1. Form groups of three or four.

2. Imagine you will meet at a class reunion ten years from now. Fill out the form below for yourself and for the other members of your group.

3. One person at a time, tell your predictions about yourself, and then listen to the others' predictions about you. Whose predictions do you think are the closest?

	About myself	Group member 1	Group member 2	Group member 3
Job/career ten years from now				
Previous jobs held				
Marital/family status				
Hobbies or interests				
Where the person now lives/has lived				
Places she or he has traveled				
Something unexpected				
Other				

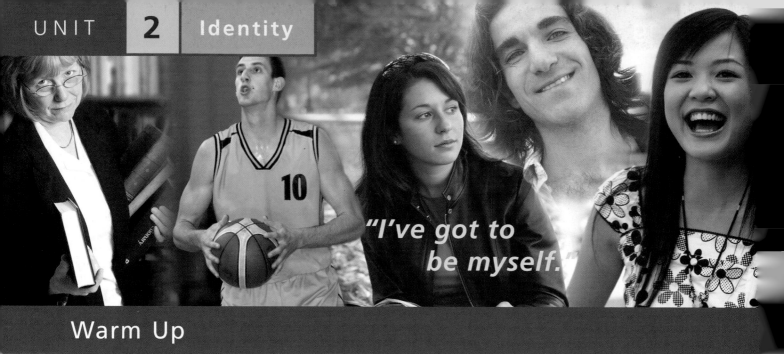

"I've got to be myself."

Warm Up

These people all have unexpected personal qualities.
Write the missing words and phrases.

nerd	fame	private	go pro
romantic	jock	make it big	
sense of humor	passionate	straight A student	

1. Ms. Kelsey is a librarian, but she's __passionate__ about sports cars.

2. Kris rides a motorcycle, but she's also a _____ when it comes to history.

3. Dave's friends thought that _____ing _____ in Hollywood would change him, but Dave is still just a regular guy. _____ hasn't changed him.

4. Jonathan might be the best basketball player in the state, but he doesn't have any dreams of _____ing _____. He just wants to play for fun.

5. Terry is a _____, but when he's not on the football field, he's watching _____ movies.

6. Everybody assumes Carrie is a serious person because she's quiet. But she's really got a great _____.

7. Jordan is very friendly and open with everyone, but she keeps some things about her life _____.

8. Mark is very intelligent, but he's not a _____. He hates to study!

Now listen and check.

CD 1, Track 10

Do you have any special traits, hobbies, or skills? Tell your partner.

USEFUL EXPRESSIONS

Did you know that I ...

I never would have guessed.

Some people aren't what they seem.

There's more to him than meets the eye.

Most people think I ...

12

Listening Task

👁 **Look at the pictures. What is each person like?**

🎧 **First Listening:** What is surprising about each person?

CD 1, Tracks 11–14

1. ☐ He plays football really well.
   ☑ He has a lot of interests outside of sports.
   ☐ He's a popular musician.

2. ☐ He has won several dance competitions.
   ☐ He doesn't think he dances very well.
   ☐ He enjoys dancing privately.

3. ☐ She isn't a nerd.
   ☐ She's in a rock band *and* she's a good student.
   ☐ She wants to quit school.

🎧 **Second Listening:** How does the other person react?

CD 1, Tracks 11–14

1.  ☐ She thinks Brett is a bad poet.
   ☑ She is surprised that Brett is romantic.

2.  ☐ He thinks Jeff should be proud of his hobby.
   ☐ He thinks Jeff's hobby is funny.

3.  ☐ He thinks rock musicians can't be good students.
   ☐ He doesn't believe that Kayla can play an instrument.

13

Real World Listening

PREPARE

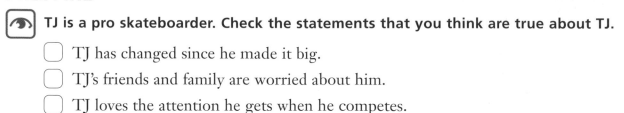

TJ is a pro skateboarder. Check the statements that you think are true about TJ.

☐ TJ has changed since he made it big.

☐ TJ's friends and family are worried about him.

☐ TJ loves the attention he gets when he competes.

Now listen and check.

CD 1, Tracks 15–16

GET THE MAIN IDEAS

Write T (true), F (false), or ? (no information) for each statement.

CD 1,
Tracks 15–16

___ TJ won first place in the Pro-Am championship.

___ TJ gets tired from signing lots of autographs.

___ TJ is doing a commercial to advertise shoes.

___ TJ's friends and family think he doesn't want to hang out with them anymore.

___ TJ thinks he is the same person he was before he went pro.

___ TJ loves having spectators watch him.

___ TJ wants to quit competing.

___ TJ wants to be true to himself.

RESPOND TO THE IDEAS

1. Does TJ fit the image you have of a professional athlete? Why or why not?
2. Are there things about you that people are surprised to learn when they get to know you better? What are they?

14

WHO ARE YOU REALLY?

1. Form groups of three to five people.

2. Take turns. Choose a box that fits an aspect of your life. Then read the box aloud.

3. Others in your group ask yes/no questions to try to guess what this aspect of your life is.

4. Continue until you have done all the boxes, or until time is up.

Something I'm good at now	Something I collect (or used to collect)	A special trip	Something I like to do with my friends	A restaurant I love
A book that taught me something special	Something active I like to do	Three verbs that say something about me	Someone who inspired me	Something I used to want to be
A job I've had	Something I like to do by myself	A dream I had when I was in high school	Something quiet I like to do	Three adjectives that say something about me
A pet	A special friendship	A talent I have (or used to have)	Something I hate having to do	Something I'm bad at (but I love doing it anyway)
Three nouns that say something about me	A home (or place) I've lived in	Something I liked doing with my family	A special place in my city	A school I attended

HINT FOR ASKING QUESTIONS:
Start with general questions and work toward more specific details.

"If you don't mind my saying so."

Warm Up

 Mabel Clarkson is an advice columnist. Read the advice she gives to her readers. Write the missing words.

Dear Mabel

possessive	spanking	tantrums
folks	blind	fix
way	stick	
blame	discipline	

1. Dear Mabel:

My four-year-old daughter has horrible <u>tantrums</u>*. How do I get her to stop crying?*

Well, you need to _____ her. Some people aren't comfortable _____ their kids. If you don't want to punish her physically, try taking away something special—maybe a toy. Whatever you do, pick one method and _____ to it. Use the same method all the time.

2.

Dear Mabel:

Whenever I start dating a new girl, my parents get in the _____. They always invite her over to talk. What should I do?

Don't _____ your _____ for being interested in your life. They care

3. about you!

Dear Mabel:

One of my friends wants to _____ me up with her neighbor. She thinks we would be a great match. Should I agree to a date even though we've never met?

_____ dates are kind of scary; you don't know what to expect. But I say: Go for it!

4.

Dear Mabel:

My boyfriend doesn't want me to spend time with my friends. What can I do about his jealousy?

Ooh … that's a bad sign. If your boyfriend is _____ now, he'll just get worse later. You should meet someone new.

🎧 **Now listen and check.**
CD 1, Track 17

Do you agree with Mabel's advice? Do you know anyone who's had these problems?

USEFUL EXPRESSIONS

It's none of your business.

If you ask me …

Don't you think it's time to … ?

It's hard to deal with …

It's a personal thing.

Listening Task

👁 **Look at the pictures. What is the situation?**

🎧 **First Listening:** What kind of advice does the person give?

1, Tracks 18–22

1

☑ Have a baby soon.
☐ Quit your job and have kids.

2

☐ Don't move back home after college.
☐ Save some money for a better place.

3

☐ Discipline the child.
☐ Don't give the child sweets when he's upset.

4

☐ Go to bars and clubs to meet someone.
☐ Make an effort to meet someone.

🎧 **Second Listening:** Why is the advice offensive or unwanted?

CD 1, Tracks 18–22

1.
☐ It isn't possible for Amy to have a child.
☑ They want to have the baby only when they are ready.

2.
☐ He knows his parents won't get in his way.
☐ He's already decided to move back home.

3.
☐ She doesn't believe in spanking.
☐ She already tried spanking and it didn't work.

4.
☐ She doesn't want to date anyone right now.
☐ She feels that no one wants to date her.

17

Real World Listening

PREPARE

 Andrea Price gives advice on the radio. What advice do you think she'll give to the callers?

PROBLEM

1. living with parents

2. trouble losing weight

3. noisy car

ADVICE

- ☐ Follow your parents' rules.
- ☐ Move out.
- ☐ Tell them the rules are unfair.

- ☐ Eat less.
- ☐ Eliminate certain foods from your diet.
- ☐ Exercise.

- ☐ Get the brakes fixed.
- ☐ Get a new car.
- ☐ Call someone else.

 Now listen and check.

CD 1, Tracks 23–26

GET THE MAIN IDEAS

 How does Andrea explain her advice?

CD 1, Tracks 23–26

Problem	Reason
Jackie: living with parents	☐ Jackie's parents have the right to set rules in their house. ☐ Jackie is too young to be responsible.
Beatrice: losing weight	☐ Beatrice has no self-control. ☐ Losing weight is more complicated than Beatrice thinks.
Pete: noisy car	☐ It would be better to consult a mechanic. ☐ The car could be dangerous.

RESPOND TO THE IDEAS

1. **Do you agree with Andrea Price's advice? Why or why not? What other suggestions would you have made?**

2. **Has anyone ever asked you for advice? What was the problem? What advice did you give? How did it end up?**

2

ADVICE COLUMN

1. **Form groups of three or four. The first person chooses one of the problems and reads it aloud to the other group members, along with the advice. If any group member has a different piece of advice, write it under "Your idea."**

2. **The group decides which advice it feels is best to follow.**

3. **Continue with a new problem.**

I'm already too busy at work, but my boss just asked me to help with a new project. I'll go crazy if I have to do it, but I don't want to look like I can't handle extra responsibility. What should I do?

~ Signed, Stressed out

Show your boss the different projects you currently have to do, and ask which one you should drop in order to take on the new project.

Your idea:

_____

_____

I just got accepted at the University of Melbourne, in Australia. My boyfriend is going to college in our home country. I don't want to live apart, but this is my chance to study abroad. What should I do?   ~ Signed, Studious but in love

Follow your dream and study in Australia. If your boyfriend really loves you, he'll wait. Absence makes the heart grow fonder.

Your idea:

_____

_____

Two different people have asked me to marry them. One is gentle, funny, and easy to get along with. The other isn't quite as nice, but he makes twice as much money and wants to take care of me. Which should I marry?   ~ Signed, Confused

It's a lot easier to get used to someone when you are financially stable. Marry the rich one!

Your idea:

_____

_____

I bought a book on how to get rich in real estate, and I found out it doesn't help at all. I feel like I was cheated, and I want my money back. When I called their office, though, they said, "Sorry, all sales are final." What can I do?   ~ Signed, Angry and broke

Sue them. That's what lawyers are for!

Your idea:

_____

_____

"I'm sure you'll get along with them."

Warm Up

 Read about the interesting characters in Jerome's family. Write the missing words and phrases.

Jerome

fanatic	freak out	relative
devoted	nuts	extreme
irritating	vegan	strict

1. My family is a little unusual. Some people might even say we're _____nuts_____.

2. My mother is _____ when it comes to neatness. She can't stand to see even a speck of dust in the house.

3. Mom is really _____ with us when it comes to household chores. Every day, we have to do a couple of hours of chores to keep things neat.

4. My father loves to barbecue. He's definitely a _____. He can't live without his barbecue grill.

5. One time, I accidentally broke Dad's grill. He completely _____ed ____. He was so upset, he couldn't even wait a day to buy another one.

6. My sister, Alicia, is a _____. She not only avoids meat, but also any animal products, like milk and eggs.

7. Sometimes Alicia and Dad argue because they have opposite interests. She's as _____ to her vegetarianism as he is to his barbecuing.

8. Some of my other _____s are a little strange, too. I've got an aunt who thinks she can see the future and a cousin who does four hours of bodybuilding exercises every day!

9. My family might be a little _____ to some people, but they don't bother me much. After all, they're the only family I've got.

 Now listen and check.

CD 1, Track 27

USEFUL EXPRESSIONS

How can I put this nicely?
The thing about him is ...
She's a fanatic about ...
He can't live without ...
Some people think she's ...

20 **Do you have any interesting characters in your family?**

👁 **Look at the pictures. What do you think the people will talk about?**

🎧 **First Listening:** **What is unusual about each person?**

1, Tracks 28–32

1

- ☑ She has a very particular diet.
- ☐ She treats her cat like a child.
- ☐ She doesn't like to eat with other people.

2

- ☐ He annoys everyone with his clown act.
- ☐ He is a clown at heart.
- ☐ He has a pet goose.

3

- ☐ She is a fanatic about her hobby.
- ☐ She has too much stuff in her apartment.
- ☐ She thinks she's perfect.

4

- ☐ He likes to imitate people.
- ☐ He likes to pretend he is a TV or movie character.
- ☐ He's crazy.

🎧 **Second Listening:** **Check the true details. (There may be more than one.)**

CD 1, Tracks 28–32

1.
- ☐ She only eats cooked vegetables.
- ☑ She makes her cat follow a vegan diet.
- ☐ She eats meat only at family gatherings.

2.
- ☐ He makes balloon hats when he's not working.
- ☐ His duck follows him everywhere.
- ☐ He wears his clown suit all the time.

3.
- ☐ She has dolls in every room.
- ☐ She has one hundred dolls.
- ☐ She keeps the dolls in their boxes.

4.
- ☐ He loves science fiction.
- ☐ His family is worried about him.
- ☐ He wears strange costumes.

21

PREPARE

 Lydia and Greg are going to get married this summer. They are preparing their wedding invitations. How many people will Lydia invite? How many will Greg invite?

 Now listen and check.

CD 1, Tracks 33–34

$\mathcal{L}\mathcal{G}$

William and Grace Chen proudly announce the marriage of their beloved first daughter

Ms. Lydia Chen

to

Mr. Gregory Parker

You are cordially invited to the wedding, which will take place at

GET THE MAIN IDEAS

 Do you agree or disagree with the statements below?
(5 = strongly agree, 1 = strongly disagree.)

CD 1,
Tracks 33–34

Greg is happy to be a new member of Lydia's family.	5	4	3	2	1
Lydia's father is very important to her.	5	4	3	2	1
Greg and Lydia have the same "family values."	5	4	3	2	1
Lydia is very happy to be part of a large family.	5	4	3	2	1
Greg and Lydia will have a successful marriage.	5	4	3	2	1

Compare answers with a partner. Explain your opinions.

 ## RESPOND TO THE IDEAS

1. Whose family is more similar to yours—Greg's or Lydia's? In what ways?
2. If you get married, how many people will you invite to your wedding? Who will you invite? Who won't you invite?

FAMILY LIES

The goal of this game is to fool your partner so that he or she cannot guess which "family facts" are real and which are lies.

1. Write something interesting, unusual, or hard to believe about four family members. One fact should be a lie—either the family member does not exist, or the information about that person is a lie.

2. Get into pairs. Introduce the members of your family and tell the interesting facts about each family member.

3. Your partner can ask ten questions about your family. After asking the ten questions, your partner has to guess which is the lie. Say whether your partner is correct or not.

OPTION: After finishing, talk about the relationships among your family members, using some of the phrases you learned in this unit.

	Name	Interesting fact
Mother (or stepmother)		
Father (or stepfather)		
Sister		
Brother		
Grandmother		
Grandfather		
Aunt		
Uncle		
Niece		
Nephew		
Daughter		
Son		

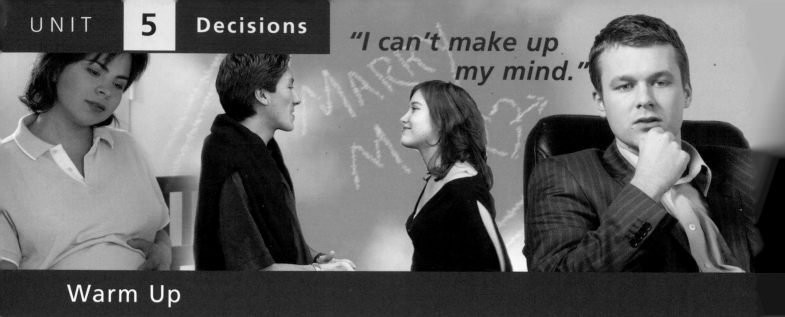

"I can't make up my mind."

Warm Up

👁 **Read about the important decisions these people are facing. Write the missing words.**

figure	major	weigh
lean	decide	downside
stay-at-home	realize	heart-to-heart

1. Pamela is pregnant with her first child. She has to decide whether she wants to be a working mom or a **stay-at-home** mom.

2. The Yamamotos are planning a vacation. They have to _____ out which airline offers the cheapest rates.

3. Stan is unhappy at work, but he makes a good salary. He's going to _____ the pros and cons of getting a lower-paying job that he likes better.

4. Kelsey is _____ing toward going to Harvard because she has family near Boston, but she also really likes Yale.

5. Ben just _____ed to propose to his girlfriend, Laura. He's going to have an airplane write "Will you marry me?" in the sky.

6. Mrs. Lai's company wants to transfer her to another country. She's going to have a _____ conversation with her husband about it tonight.

7. Katherine isn't sure whether she wants to _____ in anthropology or linguistics.

8. Jeremy and Priscilla didn't _____ until they got engaged how difficult it is to plan a wedding.

9. For Roland, the _____ of buying a new car is that he has to do lots of research to make the best decision.

🎧 **Now listen and check.**

CD 1, Track 35

👤 **Have you made decisions about any of these topics? What did you decide to do?**

24

> **USEFUL EXPRESSIONS**
>
> I'm seriously considering it.
> I'm not sure I'm ready to take that step.
> I've been thinking about it.
> I'm still undecided.
> I don't want to rush you.

Listening Task

👁 **Look at the pictures. What kind of decisions do you think they will discuss?**

🎧 **First Listening:** **What is the speaker thinking about doing?**

1, Tracks 36–40

1

- ☑ getting a job
- ☐ quitting her job
- ☐ becoming a stay-at-home mom

2

- ☐ looking for a job in another state
- ☐ accepting a new job and moving
- ☐ finding a new career

3

- ☐ choosing a major
- ☐ majoring in more than one subject
- ☐ dropping out of college

4

- ☐ getting a bigger apartment
- ☐ getting a puppy
- ☐ getting another pet

🎧 **Second Listening:** **What does the other person say?**
(There may be more than one answer.)

CD1, Tracks 36–40

1.
- ☑ No one will take care of things at home.
- ☐ Working is too stressful.
- ☐ It might be difficult to find a job.

2.
- ☐ The job is a great opportunity.
- ☐ Texas is far away.
- ☐ Six weeks from now is too soon to move.

3.
- ☐ She should major in psychology.
- ☐ She could do great things in any subject.
- ☐ She shouldn't keep changing her mind.

4.
- ☐ A puppy is messy.
- ☐ A big dog wouldn't like their little apartment.
- ☐ A cat might be a better choice for them.

25

PREPARE

 You are going to hear a presentation on decision making. There are four dimensions, or measurements, in decision making. Match the dimensions with the definitions.

1. approach _____
2. information _____
3. risk _____
4. decisiveness _____

a. how fast you make a decision and how fast you act on your decision

b. what kinds of facts and values you need to consider before deciding

c. how you deal with struggles and challenges when you face a tough decision

d. the way that you view the process of reaching a decision

Now listen and check.

CD 1, Tracks 41–42

GET THE MAIN IDEAS

Match each dimension with the two types of decision makers.

CD 1, Tracks 41–42

1. approach _____ _____

2. information _____ _____

3. risk _____ _____

4. decisiveness _____ _____

Abstract
Originators
Challengers
Organized
Concrete
Flexible
Conciliators
Adapters

RESPOND TO THE IDEAS

1. What do you think of this style of decision making? Does it make sense?

2. Tell a partner about a big decision that you had to make in your life. What were the pros and cons? What did you decide to do? What kind of "decision maker" were you when you made this decision: Originator? Challenger? Other?

GET A LIFE

1. Life is full of choices. What is important to you? Check the things in the chart that you would prefer to have in your life.

		Me	Person A	Person B
Career	Business	☐	☐	☐
	Government	☐	☐	☐
	Health care	☐	☐	☐
	Entertainment	☐	☐	☐
Education	Undergraduate degree	☐	☐	☐
	Graduate degree	☐	☐	☐
Location	Rural	☐	☐	☐
	Suburban	☐	☐	☐
	Urban	☐	☐	☐
Housing	Old house	☐	☐	☐
	New apartment	☐	☐	☐
Marital Status	Married	☐	☐	☐
	Single	☐	☐	☐
	Divorced	☐	☐	☐
Spouse/significant other	Beautiful	☐	☐	☐
	Intelligent	☐	☐	☐
Children	0	☐	☐	☐
	1	☐	☐	☐
	2	☐	☐	☐
	3	☐	☐	☐
	10	☐	☐	☐
Pets	Cat	☐	☐	☐
	Dog	☐	☐	☐
	Fish	☐	☐	☐
	None	☐	☐	☐

2. Now talk to two classmates. Find out what is important to them. Discuss the things you think are important. Give reasons for your opinions and preferences.

PART 1. Hearing the correct words.

Listen and write the missing words.

CD 1, Track 43

1. After our band got some popularity, we _____, and now we're each going our own way.

2. I've just realized what my _____ is. I'm going to be a radio announcer!

3. My parents hope my brother will _____ them in the noodle shop, but he wants to be a pro golfer.

4. You would assume that Carrie wasn't a very good student, since she's such a star tennis player, but she's _____.

5. Manny acts like a _____ at school, but you ought to see him on the dance floor!

6. Everyone who ever picks up a guitar dreams of _____, but most never even get a chance.

7. I thought Michael would give up poetry within a month, but he's really _____.

8. My boyfriend is so _____. He won't even let me join a study group if there's another guy in it.

9. She has a _____ if I smile and say "hi" to someone else.

10. My mother's a real _____ about Korean TV dramas. She never misses an episode.

11. My brother is insanely _____ to Seattle Mariners baseball.

12. He was watching a game, and when I asked to see my favorite program, he completely _____.

13. I'm glad to see Michelle so happy with her new boyfriend, but the _____ is that she never has time for her friends anymore.

14. If you can't make up your mind about which bicycle to buy, try _____ of each type.

15. Right now, I'm _____ taking biology class, but I kind of want to take photography instead.

PART 2. Understanding conversations.

🎧 **Listen to each conversation. Then circle the answers.**

CD 1, Tracks 44–53

1. Where is Terry learning to be a chef?

   (a) At a university

   (b) From an apprentice

   (c) At his family's restaurant

   (d) At cooking school

2. How does Kate describe Cindy now?

   (a) So normal

   (b) Such a free spirit

   (c) A judge

   (d) Having crazy hair

3. What does Kayla's friend want?

   (a) Tickets to her band's performance

   (b) Her math notes

   (c) Her English notes

   (d) Drum lessons

4. What does Katie's friend think of Brett?

   (a) He's romantic.

   (b) He's a great poet.

   (c) He's a jock.

   (d) He's really handsome.

5. Why is Jerry moving in with his parents?

   (a) He can't find his own apartment.

   (b) He likes to spend time with them.

   (c) He misses them.

   (d) He wants to save money.

6. What advice does Lucie's friend offer?

   (a) Go out and look for a date.

   (b) Get some chocolate ice cream.

   (c) Get some rest.

   (d) Stay at home.

7. Why is the sister a vegan?

   (a) For religious reasons

   (b) For health reasons

   (c) To keep her cat healthy

   (d) For no real reason

8. How does Andrew's brother feel about Andrew acting like TV characters?

   (a) He doesn't care.

   (b) He thinks it's extreme.

   (c) He thinks it's normal.

   (d) He thinks it's always funny.

9. What does the woman do now?

   (a) She works in an office.

   (b) She teaches at a high schoool.

   (c) She's a stay-at-home mom.

   (d) She's in high school.

10. Why does the woman want a puppy?

   (a) It would keep the neighbor's cat away.

   (b) A puppy is messy.

   (c) A puppy is so cute.

   (d) It's free at the supermarket.

"It's hard to understand h... sometimes."

Warm Up

 Two students are studying English as a second language. Read their opinions. Choose the correct words.

Young-Hae

1. I think teachers who work in the United States and the UK should be ☑ **native** ☐ **homeland** speakers of English.

2. There are so many varieties of English that I can never be an ☑ **expert** ☐ **professional** in all of them.

3. English has a lot of ☑ **slang** ☐ **fluency**. How am I supposed to know that a "hot" pair of jeans means the same thing as a "cool" pair of jeans?

4. I would be worried about ☐ **approaching** ☑ **applying** for a job in the United States. What if they didn't think my English was good enough?

June

5. I don't mind if my teacher has a different ☐ **communication** ☑ **accent** than I'm used to, as long as I can understand what he or she is saying.

6. I think it's useful to have some knowledge of different ☑ **dialects** ☐ **standards** of English. That knowledge will ☐ **handle** ☑ **come in handy** when I travel.

7. The large number of slang words in English is ☑ **amazing** ☐ **incredulous**. There is a lot to ☐ **pick up** ☑ **take out**!

8. I think companies should ☐ **rent** ☑ **hire** non-native speakers of English if they are qualified to do the job.

 Now listen and check.

CD 1, Track 54

Which of these ideas do you agree with? What kinds of English have you heard? Talk about your experiences with a partner.

32

USEFUL EXPRESSIONS

It's hard to pick up ...

I think it's useful to ...

She has a heavy accent.

I need to work on my accent.

I have a hard time understanding ...

👁 **Look at the pictures. Where are the people?**

🎧 **First Listening:**
CD 1, Tracks 55–58
What are the people talking about?

1. _____

2. _____

3. _____

🎧 **Second Listening:**
CD 1, Tracks 55–58
Write T (true) or F (false).

1. ___ People use different vocabulary in different countries.

___ "Mozzie" means "most."

___ "Tucker" means "food."

2. ___ Everyone has an accent.

___ It's hard to get used to some accents.

___ Some people don't have an accent.

3. ___ Accents are different even in the same country.

___ "R" sounds are dropped in the American South.

___ "I" sounds are dropped in the American South.

SUMI WILSO

2320 Everglades Drive | Miami, FL 74354 | (305) 55

Work Experience
Sales Manager
Tokyo East Travel World
Tokyo, Japan

Education
B.A., Travel Industry Management
University of Florida

PREPARE

Sumi has a degree in travel management. She's applying for a job at World Trek travel agency in New York. What job do you think she's applying for?

- [ ] Tour guide
- [ ] Customer service representative
- [ ] Department manager
- [ ] Secretary
- [ ] Security guard
- [ ] Another position _____

Do you think she will get the job?

- [ ] Yes
- [ ] No

Now listen and check.

CD 1, Tracks 59–62

GET THE MAIN IDEAS

Answer these questions.

CD 1, Tracks 59–62

1. What job did Sumi apply for? _____

2. What qualifications does she have? _____

3. What job was Sumi offered? _____

4. Why does Sumi think she was offered that job?

_____

5. What is Sumi going to do? _____

RESPOND TO THE IDEAS

1. **Do you think Sumi made the right decision? What would you have done?**

2. **Are there any jobs that can only be done by native speakers? What jobs? Why?**

34

Interaction Link

ENGLISH OR ENGLISHES?

1. **Read the opinions about English and add two new ideas of your own.**

2. **Walk around the classroom and ask different classmates questions to fill in the chart. When you find someone who agrees with one of the statements, find out why. If you disagree, argue in favor of your viewpoint.**

3. **Make groups of three or four and share the answers you got. Discuss any ideas that you have strong opinions about.**

Find someone who believes ...	Name	Why do they think so?
American English should be the standard taught worldwide.		
Our native accents, when speaking English, are an important part of our identities.		
English is the property of native speakers—everyone else is just borrowing it.		
Only native speakers should teach English.		
You can learn as much, or more, by speaking English with other non-native speakers.		
[your idea]		
[your idea]		

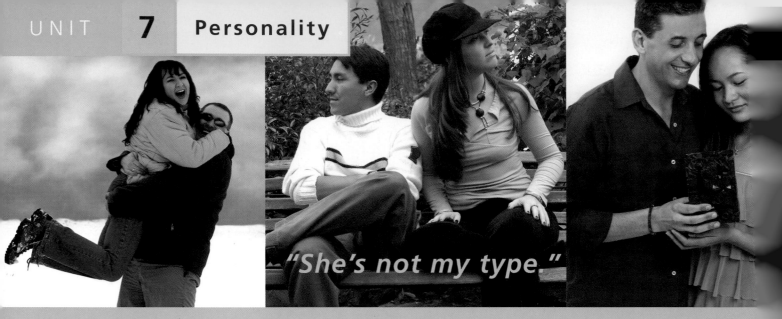

"She's not my type."

Warm Up

Read these statements about choosing a mate. Write the missing words and phrases.

warm up to	fall for	blown away	sensitive	commitment
click	attractive	income	quality time	

1. The guy has to be **attractive** or I won't date him.

2. I don't need to be _____ by the girl's looks, but she should have a nice smile.

3. I like to spend money, so I need someone with a good _____.

4. It takes me a few months to _____ people. But then I start to feel comfortable with them.

5. I can usually tell within the first few minutes of meeting someone whether or not we _____.

6. I want a guy who's _____. He should consider my feelings and opinions.

7. I tend to _____ women who have a sense of humor.

8. I'm not interested in making a _____ at this point in my life. I just want to have fun!

9. I don't want somebody who's so busy with work that he can't spend _____ with me.

Now listen and check.

CD 1, Track 63

Do you agree with any of these statements? What do you look for in a mate?

USEFUL EXPRESSIONS

She might be "the one."
We just "click."
She's not my type.
It was love at first sight.
He's my "knight in shining armor."

👁 **Look at the pictures. What do you think these people are like?**

🎧 **First Listening:** **What do these people say about themselves?**

1, Tracks 64–68

1

Age: ⬭

Marital status: ⬭

Hobbies: ⬭

2

Age: ⬭

Employer: ⬭

Interests: ⬭

3

Age: ⬭

Personality: ⬭

Hobbies: ⬭

4

Age: ⬭

Background: ⬭

Interests: ⬭

🎧 **Second Listening:** **What kind of person is each speaker looking for?**
Check the correct answers. (There may be more than one.)

CD 1, Tracks 64–68

1.
- ☐ a casual relationship
- ☐ a long-term partner
- ☐ a fun person

2.
- ☐ an independent person
- ☐ a relaxed person
- ☐ an honest person

3.
- ☐ a good cook
- ☐ a rich person
- ☐ a casual relationship

4.
- ☐ a soldier
- ☐ an intelligent person
- ☐ a beach bum

PREPARE

👁 **Amy and Luis are talking to their friends about each other.**

What do you think Amy likes about Luis?	What do you think Luis likes about Amy?
☐ He's handsome.	☐ She's thin.
☐ He's not too tall.	☐ She's athletic.
☐ He dresses very well.	☐ She's attractive.
☐ He's funny.	☐ She's well educated.
☐ He's an athlete.	☑ She's independent.

🎧 **Now listen and check.**

CD 1, Tracks 69–71

GET THE MAIN IDEAS

🎧 **Which of these statements describe Luis? Which ones describe Amy?**

CD 1,
Tracks 69–71

Luis

☐ He looks like a Greek statue.	☐ He doesn't dress well.
☐ He's Amy's type.	☐ He's sweet and funny.
☐ He's got big hands.	☐ He's easy to be with.

Amy

☐ She's romantic	☐ She's aggressive.
☐ She's Luis's type.	☐ She waited for Luis to ask her out.
☐ She's thin.	☑ She's independent.

RESPOND TO THE IDEAS

1. **How did Luis and Amy's ideas about each other change over time?**

2. **What things are important to you when you first meet someone? What things do you want in a person you spend your life with? Are they the same? Why or why not?**

MATCHMAKERS

1. Fill in the chart below to create your own dating profile.

DATING PROFILE

Age _____   Residence _____

Occupation _____   Salary _____

Likes/dislikes about the job _____

Height _____   Weight _____   Body type _____

Personality (good and bad points) _____

Hobbies _____

Preferences	Favorite	Least Favorite
Music		
Movies		
Reading material		
TV programs		
Sports		
Food		
Clothing		
Favorite places to go on a date		
A perfect date		

2. Interview a partner and write a profile for him or her.

"Operate with caution."

Warm Up

 Read this magazine article about modern technology. Write the missing words and phrases.

identity theft	obsession	incompatible	updates
delete	forwards	clogged up	
viruses	addictive	spam	

MODERN TECHNOLOGY: FRIEND OR FOE?

Modern technology has made our lives easier. But have we traded convenience for danger? Let's take a look at the dark side of technology:

1. *Hidden Expenses:* Better save up some cash. Program developers are constantly changing their software, and you may need to pay to get the newest __updates__. Getting ready to buy a new computer? You might find that the programs you already own are _____ with your new system.

2. *Security:* The Internet has made shopping easy. But it is possible to steal online credit information. That's why insurance companies are offering _____ policies. You also have to worry about _____ that could damage your computer.

3. *Privacy:* Many people couldn't live without e-mail. But most people could live without _____. Your inbox can get so _____ with cyber junk mail that you spend all your time _____ing it. And what about those "cute" _____ people send? They might seem funny to some people, but they're annoying to most.

4. *Mental Health:* Computers are very entertaining, but have people become too attached? For some, the computer has become an _____. Video games and online gambling are _____ activities that can make you a prisoner of your computer.

Now listen and check.
CD 1, Track 72

USEFUL EXPRESSIONS
You have to worry about ...
It's a bad influence.
I can't live without ...
It lets you get out your frustrations.
I'm hooked on ...

Have you had any of the problems the article describes? Do you think the positives of computers outweigh the negatives?

Listening Task

👁 **Look at the pictures. What problems do these people have with their computers?**

🎧 **First Listening:**

CD 1, Tracks 73–77

Why is the speaker complaining about computers?

1.

2.

3.

4.

🎧 **Second Listening:**

CD 1, Tracks 73–77

Which statement do you think the speaker would agree with?

1. ☐ People shouldn't use their credit cards over the internet.
   ☐ Websites should take additional security measures to protect buyers.

2. ☐ Software companies should offer more free or low cost upgrades.
   ☐ Software companies should upgrade programs less frequently so buyers don't need to repurchase constantly.

3. ☐ E-mail should be used only for serious communication.
   ☐ People should think more carefully before forwarding lots of jokes and funny pictures.

4. ☐ Video games can become an obsession.
   ☐ Video games cause people to become lazy and violent.

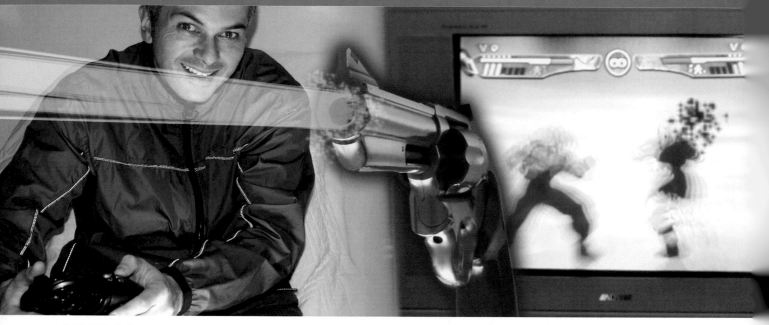

PREPARE

 Jeff Townsend is a video game developer. He's on *Tech Trek* to discuss his new video game "The Butcher."

What do you think Jeff will say about "The Butcher"?

☐ It's fun.

☐ It helps to prevent violence.

☐ It causes people to become violent.

☐ It's a good lesson for children.

🎧 **Now listen and check.**

CD 1, Tracks 78–79

GET THE MAIN IDEAS

🎧 **Check the statements that Jeff believes.**

CD 1, Tracks 78–79

☐ Violent video games should be played only by adults.

☐ "The Butcher" isn't as bloody as some people say it is.

☐ Video games are just entertainment.

☐ People are smart enough to understand the difference between fantasy and real life.

☐ No one is going to try to imitate the Butcher.

☐ You'll be more relaxed if you play the game.

☐ It is better to let out your anger and frustration in a fantasy game than in real life.

☐ The game encourages people to become cops.

☐ People can't get a real addiction to video games.

RESPOND TO THE IDEAS

1. **Do you agree with Jeff? Why or why not? Which of his points do you think is the strongest? Which is the weakest?**

2. **What do you think of all the new forms of entertainment made possible by computers? What are some of the negative and positive effects?**

TECHNOLOGICAL ISSUES

1. Answer the questions about technology.

2. Ask a partner the same questions. Discuss your opinions.

Issue	Me	My partner
Do video games cause violence?		
Where is it acceptable or unacceptable to talk on a cell phone?		
Is it OK to break up with a boyfriend or girlfriend by e-mail?		
Is it OK to meet an online friend in person?		
Is it safe to buy things on the Internet with a credit card?		
Should downloading music and movies be legal or illegal? Why?		

"She's got some unusual habits."

Warm Up

 Krista has just started her first year of college. She has some new problems dealing with roommates and family. Write the missing words.

space	dormitory	appreciative	snore	annoying
curfew	concerned	barge in	negatives	

1. Now that Krista is in college, she doesn't live at home. She lives in a ___dormitory___ with other students.

2. Krista likes some of her new responsibilities, but she also thinks that college life has some major ___negatives___.

3. One problem is that the students have a 10:00 p.m. ___curfew___ on weeknights.

4. Another problem is that Krista's roommate, Jasmine, has some ___annoying___ habits. For example, she leaves her books and clothes all over the floor.

5. Jasmine also ___snore___s when she sleeps, so Krista has trouble sleeping.

6. The worst part of dorm life is there isn't much privacy. Sometimes Krista's neighbors just ___barge in___ without knocking on the door.

7. Krista also had problems with her parents. When she first moved out, they called her every day. They were ___concerned___ about their daughter.

8. At first, Krista was very ___appreciative___ that her parents cared about her. But after a while, she wanted more freedom and more privacy.

9. Now, Krista's parents only call once or twice a month. They want to give her some ___space___.

 Now listen and check.

CD 2, Track 1

 Do you live with a roommate or your family? What are those people like? Do you have any complaints?

44

Look at the pictures. What problems do you think these people have?

First Listening: What does the speaker complain about? (There may be more than one complaint.)

CD 2, Tracks 2–6

1

- ☐ messy bathroom
- ☐ curfew
- ☐ noisy neighbors
- ☐ expensive meals

2

- ☐ parents go into his room
- ☐ mom checks the phone bill
- ☐ mom uses his cell phone
- ☐ mom cleans his room

3

- ☐ snoring
- ☐ sleepwalking
- ☐ messiness
- ☐ neatness

4

- ☐ borrowing things
- ☐ breaking things
- ☐ eating things
- ☐ stealing things

Second Listening: What solution is suggested?

CD 2, Tracks 2–6

1.
   - ☐ Put up with it.
   - ☐ Move out next year.

2.
   - ☐ Get used to it.
   - ☐ There is no solution.

3.
   - ☐ Get used to it.
   - ☐ Get a divorce.

4.
   - ☐ Be more respectful.
   - ☐ Share everything.

PREPARE

Kara rents an apartment from the Johnsons, an elderly couple. Write + for things Kara probably likes about her living situation and – for things that she probably doesn't like.

☐ The Johnsons are concerned about Kara.

☐ Mrs. Johnson visits Kara in her apartment.

☐ Mrs. Johnson makes Kara home-cooked meals.

☐ Mrs. Johnson asks Kara questions about her plans.

☐ Mr. Johnson is affectionate with Kara.

☐ Something else?

_____

Now listen and check.

CD 2, Tracks 7–8

GET THE MAIN IDEAS

Why does the Johnsons' behavior bother Kara?

CD 2, Tracks 7–8

Mrs. Johnson visits every day.	☐ Her privacy is being violated. ☐ Mrs. Johnson steals things.
Mrs. Johnson brings homemade soup.	☐ Mrs. Johnson is a terrible cook. ☐ It makes her feel like a child.
Mrs. Johnson asks where she's going.	☐ She feels like she's being watched. ☐ She doesn't want her to know.
Mr. Johnson is affectionate.	☐ It makes her uncomfortable. ☐ She doesn't like him.

RESPOND TO THE IDEAS

1. Kara complains about several problems she has with the Johnsons. Which of her problems would bother you? Which wouldn't? Why?

2. Have you ever lived with annoying roommates? OR have you lived in a situation where you didn't have much privacy? How did you feel about it? What did you do?

MAJOR NEGATIVES AND MAJOR POSITIVES

1. Write something positive (+) and something negative (–) about each of the living situations in the chart.

2. Ask a partner what he or she thinks is good or bad about each situation.

	Me	My partner
Living alone +		
–		
Living with roommates +		
–		
Living with family +		
–		
Living in a retirement home +		
–		
Living in a dorm +		
–		
Living overseas +		
–		
Living in the neighborhood you grew up in +		
–		

"I feel lucky to be alive."

Warm Up

Read the information about different kinds of disasters.
Choose the correct words and phrases.

Tsunami

Sometimes there is very little warning before a tsunami. People may have only a short time to
☐ **evacuate** ☐ **evaluate** their homes. Sudawan and her family lost their home in the big tsunami
that hit Thailand. They had to move into an emergency ☐ **shelter** ☐ **hotel** for many months.

Earthquake

In a quake you might feel a rolling motion or a ☐ **sharp jolt** ☐ **high voltage**. Juan Gutierrez's
apartment building ☐ **dropped** ☐ **collapsed** in the 1985 Mexico City earthquake. Luckily, he was
able to dig himself out of the ☐ **rubble** ☐ **leftovers**. "The whole experience was ☐ **afraid**
☐ **terrifying**," he told reporters.

Avalanche

Mountain climbing can be very dangerous when there is an avalanche. Climbers can be ☐ **knocked**
☐ **fell** down the mountain. A few years ago, emergency teams risked their lives to ☐ **rescue**
☐ **solicit** survivors of a big avalanche in the Colorado Rockies.

Volcanic Eruption

The force of a volcanic eruption can ☐ **rip** ☐ **dig** trees out of the ground. After the eruption,
hot ☐ **fires** ☐ **ashes** cover the ground. The villagers on the Indonesian island of Java have
learned to accept that volcanic eruptions are a natural part of life. "There is nothing we can do to
stop them," a villager named Sukarno said.
"When we learn to ☐ **surrender to** ☐ **predict**
the volcano, we learn to be at peace with nature."

Now listen and check.

CD 2, Track 9

What other disasters do you know about?
Do you know anyone who has lived through
one? Talk about it with a partner.

USEFUL EXPRESSIONS

The next thing I knew ...
It sounds like you beat the odds.
What an ordeal!
It was a miracle.
I take it one day at a time.

👁 **Look at the pictures. What disaster is occurring? Write the disasters.**

earthquake   avalanche   volcanic eruption

🎧 CD 2, Tracks 10–13
First Listening:
What was the speaker doing when the disaster occurred?

1. ☐ camping
   ☐ mountain climbing
   ☐ skiing

2. ☐ hiking
   ☐ camping
   ☐ cutting down trees

3. ☐ sleeping
   ☐ eating dinner
   ☐ playing outside her apartment building

🎧 CD 2, Tracks 10–13
Second Listening:
How did the speaker survive?

1. ☐ His friends carried him to safety.
   ☐ He slowly climbed down the mountain.

2. ☐ She walked through hot ashes to get help.
   ☐ She made a shelter and stayed there until a helicopter came.

3. ☐ She dug herself out of the rubble.
   ☐ Someone rescued her.

Real World Listening

PREPARE

👁 **Petra Nemcova is a supermodel who survived a tsunami. What do you think she will mention?**

☐ She almost drowned.

☐ Pieces of trees and buildings crushed her.

☐ She was burned.

☐ She had to wait many hours before she was rescued.

☐ She had to evacuate her home.

☐ Her parents died.

☐ She was in the hospital in a foreign country.

☐ She had to learn to walk again.

🎧 **Now listen and check.**

CD 2, Tracks 14–15

GET THE MAIN IDEAS

🎧 **Write T (true), F (false), or ? (I don't know) for each statement.**

CD 2, Tracks 14–15

1. _____ Petra was on a trip to Thailand when the tsunami hit.

2. _____ Petra ran out of the bungalow when she saw the waves coming.

3. _____ Wood and metal hit Petra's legs.

4. _____ Petra's fiancé, Simon, pulled her above the water so that she wouldn't drown.

5. _____ Petra waited on top of a palm tree for eight hours.

6. _____ People came and took Petra out of the tree.

7. _____ Petra spent several months in the hospital.

8. _____ Petra will never be able to walk again.

9. _____ Petra plans to return to Thailand.

RESPOND TO THE IDEAS

1. **What do you think was the scariest part of Petra's ordeal?**

2. **Have you or anyone you know ever been in a disaster? How did they get through it? How did they feel about it afterward? Did it affect their life in any way?**

50

Interaction Link

BE PREPARED

1. **What do you do to keep yourself safe? Look at the scenarios below and write the things you would do to keep yourself safe.**

2. **Ask a partner how he or she would stay safe.**

You're on the beach and you see a huge wave.

My answer: _____

My partner's answer: _____

You're in a tall building and everything starts to shake.

My answer: _____

My partner's answer: _____

It's the middle of the night, you're in bed, and you smell smoke.

My answer: _____

My partner's answer: _____

You're hiking in the mountains and snow begins to fall heavily.

My answer: _____

My partner's answer: _____

You're on a boat and there's only enough food and water for a day.

My answer: _____

My partner's answer: _____

PART 1. Hearing the correct words.

Listen and write the missing words.

CD 2, Track 16

1. Knowing a second language can really _____ if you want a job in the travel industry.

2. I was surprised to find out how many different _____ there are just for American English!

3. Did you hear? Tracie's family is _____ a job as a host family.

4. Erin is really good-looking, but I was really _____ by her generosity.

5. Don't you realize that getting a puppy is a fifteen-year _____?

6. From the first time we met, somehow we just _____.

7. Watching *anime* on TV has become a bit of an _____ for you, hasn't it!

8. I was so depressed when I found out the new game I got is _____ with my computer.

9. Ahhhh! All these messages asking me to buy new software are _____
my inbox!

10. Mom, do you have to _____ my room whenever I'm on the phone
with Marsha?

11. It's really _____ when you borrow my books without asking.

12. After Kara and Ryan had their big fight, she decided to _____.

13. After the big fire in the apartment building, we had to spend a week in a _____.

14. When the typhoon came, over 80,000 families had to _____ the city.

15. My neighbor's home _____ in the earthquake, but somehow our home was safe.

PART 2. Understanding conversations.

Listen to each conversation. Then circle the answers.
CD 2, Tracks 17–26

1. What does the woman say to defend Professor Lee?
   (a) Everyone has an accent.
   (b) Professor Lee has a hearing problem.
   (c) Professor Lee doesn't have an accent at all.
   (d) Everyone is hard to understand.

2. Why is Julia trying to imitate an accent?
   (a) She's moving to a different part of the country.
   (b) She's playing a part in a play.
   (c) She thinks it sounds sexy.
   (d) She thinks it sounds funny.

3. Which is true about Michael?
   (a) He's been married before.
   (b) He prefers quiet time at home.
   (c) He wants someone to teach him to surf.
   (d) He's in his early twenties.

4. What age of man would be best for Anita?
   (a) 24
   (b) 54
   (c) 38
   (d) 63

5. How did the woman find out that someone else got her credit card number?
   (a) The police told her.
   (b) The insurance company told her.
   (c) Her credit card bill had purchases she never made.
   (d) She found out on the internet.

6. What does the woman do with forwarded joke messages?

(a) Sends them to co-workers

(b) Deletes them

(c) Reads them

(d) Prints them out

7. Which one of these things is not mentioned about the man's parents?

(a) They follow him when he goes out.

(b) They barge into his room.

(c) They look through his phone bill.

(d) They call his friends' phone numbers.

8. What is Kim's complaint about Anthony?

(a) He's a neat freak.

(b) He's messy.

(c) He works too much.

(d) She has no complaints.

9. How did the experience affect the speaker?

(a) It irritated him.

(b) It killed him.

(c) It made him crazy.

(d) It changed his life.

10. Why couldn't the speaker get out of the hole?

(a) Her arms were broken.

(b) Her legs were broken.

(c) She was unconscious.

(d) It was too deep.

"I'm not sure what he actually does."

Warm Up

👁 **Read these statements about work environments. Write the missing words and phrases.**

"Casual Friday"	business attire	cubicle
snap	get away with	force on
uptight	sloppy	startled

1. There aren't enough offices at our company for everyone, so one big room is divided into small areas. Each worker has a _____.

2. The company requires that all employees wear _____ to work. The men have to wear suits and the women have to wear suits or nice dresses.

3. The dress code is strict, but there's one day a week when we don't have to worry about it. I really look forward to _____.

4. The dress code at my last job was very relaxed all the time. My first day on the job I was really _____ to see what people were wearing. I didn't expect them to dress so informally.

5. Some people feel that what you wear to work is very important. If you dress in a messy way, people may think your work is _____, too. If you dress well, they may think your work is good, too.

6. My boss has a lot of opinions that we don't agree with. Unfortunately, he tries to _____ them _____ us. He wants us to think the same way he does.

7. I'm getting really tired of my co-worker Bob. If he keeps talking so much, I'm going to get angry and then I may _____. I might start yelling at him.

8. My boss is very _____ about being on time. She gets angry when we get to work ten minutes late.

9. My boss watches us very carefully. I can't _get away with_ anything.

🎧 **Now listen and check.**

CD 2, Track 27

What kind of work environment do you like?

56

> **USEFUL EXPRESSIONS**
> They should let us ...
> The company should require ...
> Men and women should be ...
> A dress code is / isn't necessary because ...
> I'd like to be my own boss.

Listening Task

👁 **Look at the pictures. What do you think the people are like at work?**

🎧 CD 2, Tracks 28–31 **First Listening:**
Check the details the speaker mentions. (There may be more than one.)

1. ☐ He made his employees sharpen his pencils.
   ☐ His research was not good.
   ☐ He left work early.

2. ☐ She ate all the time.
   ☐ She liked to make junk food.
   ☐ Her cookies tasted bad.

3. ☐ The company's dress code is "business attire."
   ☐ The employees should never dress casually.
   ☐ She wears jeans, T-shirts, and sweatpants to work.

🎧 CD 2, Tracks 28–31 **Second Listening:**
What is the speaker's main point?

1.  ☐ He was arrogant and didn't do any work.
   ☐ He didn't know how to do the simplest tasks.

2. ☐ She makes everyone eat too much.
   ☐ She makes everyone feel guilty if they don't eat her snacks.

3. ☐ She doesn't look professional.
   ☐ She's not fashionable.

PREPARE

 Steve is working at a company in Japan.

What problems do you think Steve will mention about his work environment?

- ◯ eating habits
- ◯ schedule
- ◯ dress code
- ◯ social customs
- ◯ following rules
- ◯ language

What complaints do you think his boss, Mr. Takahashi, will make about Steve?

- ◯ He doesn't dress appropriately.
- ◯ He drinks too much.
- ◯ He doesn't bow.
- ◯ He behaves too informally with clients.
- ◯ His work is not good.
- ◯ He's late.

 Now listen and check.

CD 2, Tracks 32–34

GET THE MAIN IDEAS

 What does Steve think about his work environment? What does Mr. Takahashi think? Write T (true), F (false), or ? (I don't know).

CD 2,
Tracks 32–34

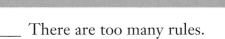

Steve thinks ...

___ There are too many rules.

___ Bowing customs are confusing.

___ The dress code is too formal.

___ People can't relax because of all the rules.

___ The other employees act rude to Mr. Takahashi.

Mr. Takahashi thinks ...

___ Steve does good work.

___ Steve looks sloppy.

___ Steve leaves too early.

___ Steve doesn't get along with the other employees.

___ Steve doesn't pay attention to his clients.

 ## RESPOND TO THE IDEAS

1. **Which style of working do you prefer: Steve's or Mr. Takahashi's?**
2. **Have you ever had an unusual or difficult boss or co-worker? Describe the situation.**

OFFICE RULES

1. What is acceptable behavior in a working environment? Check your opinions in the chart.

	OK	Not OK
Getting to the office late	☐	☐
Eating at your desk	☐	☐
Drinking beer at lunch	☐	☐
Wearing casual clothes	☐	☐
Smoking in the break room	☐	☐
Sleeping at your desk	☐	☐
Telling dirty jokes	☐	☐
Wearing perfume	☐	☐
Making personal phone calls	☐	☐
Writing personal e-mails	☐	☐

2. Work with a group. Write a list of rules for an ideal office.
It's OK to ...
It's not OK to ...

"You may need to change your routine."

Warm Up

👁 **Read about these habits. Choose the correct words and phrases.**

1. It's definitely not going to be easy to ☐ **kick** ☐ **push** my ten-year-old smoking habit!

2. When changing your diet, it's best to make ☐ **increasing** ☐ **gradual** changes.

3. Ninety-five kilos! I guess I'm going to have to stop eating at McDonald's—no more ☐ **health food** ☑ **fast food**!

4. My co-worker and I enjoy learning juicy ☐ **gossip** ☐ **chitchat** about the other employees.

5. I think my children need to ☐ **cut off** ☐ **cut down** on the time they spend talking to their friends on the phone.

6. It's rude to talk when someone else is talking. But sometimes it's hard not to ☐ **intersect** ☐ **interrupt**.

7. My best friend loves to listen in on other people's conversations. She can't stop ☐ **eavesdropping** ☐ **investigating**!

8. I often ☐ **scold** ☐ **complain** my daughter for biting her fingernails.

9. I've heard of people being ☐ **addicted in** ☐ **addicted to** smoking or alcohol. Maybe I have the same problem with chocolate!

10. I can't stand it when people talk on their cell phones in ☐ **public** ☐ **publicity**.

🎧 **Now listen and check.**

CD 2, Track 35

> USEFUL EXPRESSIONS
>
> It really bothers me when ...
>
> I wish people ...
>
> I can't stand it when ...
>
> It's rude to ...
>
> ... drives me nuts!

60 **What bad habits bother you? Share your thoughts with a partner.**

Listening Task

👁 **Look at the pictures. What is each person's bad habit?**

🎧 **First Listening:** What is the listener's attitude in each conversation?

2, Tracks 36–40

☐ He wants his friend to stop listening to private conversations.

☐ He wants to hear the details of Mark and Sarah's breakup.

☐ She's upset that her husband isn't listening to her.

☐ She's annoyed that her husband keeps talking while she is trying to tell a story.

☐ He thinks Jill is acting childish.

☐ He doesn't want Jill to be nervous.

☐ They think he's being rude.

☐ They are embarrassed that they can hear his private conversation.

🎧 **Second Listening:** What comments are made about the bad habit at the end of the conversation? Complete each sentence.

CD 2, Tracks 36–40

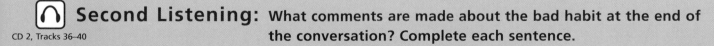

1. You've got to …
   _____

2. I didn't even realize …
   _____

3. I just hope you're not …
   _____

4. Do you think …
   _____

Real World Listening

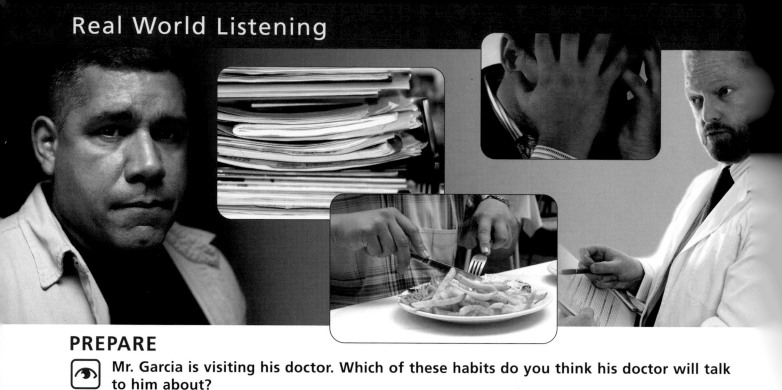

PREPARE

 Mr. Garcia is visiting his doctor. Which of these habits do you think his doctor will talk to him about?

- ☐ smoking
- ☐ eating fast food
- ☐ not exercising
- ☐ working too hard
- ☐ drinking alcohol
- ☐ drinking coffee
- ☐ yelling at his employees
- ☐ not sleeping enough
- ☐ another habit _____

Now listen and check.

CD 2, Tracks 41–43

GET THE MAIN IDEAS

What excuses does Mr. Garcia give to Dr. Morrissey?

CD 2, Track 42

Dr. Morrissey's suggestions	Mr. Garcia's excuses
• diet	_____
• exercise	_____
• relaxation	_____

What changes does Mr. Garcia make?

CD 2, Track 43

Bad habits	Changes
• eating badly	_____
• not exercising	_____
• working too much	_____

RESPOND TO THE IDEAS

1. Which of the doctor's suggestions do you think is the most important for Mr. Garcia to do?

2. Have you ever made an important life change by stopping a bad habit? How?

2

KICKING THE HABIT

1. Read the bad habits in the chart. What's the best way to "kick" each habit?

2. Ask a partner how he or she would kick each habit.

3. As a class, vote on the most effective methods.

	My idea	My partner's idea
Eating too much junk food		
Drinking too much coffee		
Cracking my knuckles		
Being a shopaholic		
Smoking		
Biting my fingernails		
Playing with my hair		
Picking my nose		
Sucking my thumb		
Other: _____		

"Getting there is
half the fun."

Warm Up

👁 **Read about Tim and Mindy's trip to the Australian Outback. Write the missing words.**

persistent	refused	trek	stranded	insisted	back
cheat	booked	realized	advance	soaked	

1. We decided to go on a three-day ___trek___ in the Australian Outback.

2. The tour guide required that we pay in ___advance___ for the tour.

3. Later, we found out that the guide had changed the location of the tour. We thought he was trying to ___cheat___ us.

4. He ___refused___ to take us to the places where we had planned to go on the tour. He said the conditions were too difficult, but we were sure we could handle it.

5. We were going to ask for our money back and just get another guide. But all the other tours were already ___booked___.

6. So we kept arguing with the tour guide for half an hour. We were very ___persistent___.

7. We ___insisted___ that he take us where we wanted. He finally agreed to do it.

8. The first day of the trip the tour guide took us into an area where it was raining heavily. We got completely ___soaked___.

9. By the second day of the trip, we were exhausted and moving slowly. We were worried that the tour guide might leave us behind and that we would be ___stranded___ in the middle of the wilderness.

10. We didn't think we were going to make it ___back___ to the hotel, but we finally did.

11. We ___realized___ that we should have listened to the tour guide. It's too bad when you make a fool of yourself in a foreign country, but at least we learned a lesson!

🎧 **Now listen and check.**

CD 2, Track 44

USEFUL EXPRESSIONS

It turned out to be a great experience!

I took him up on the offer.

It never showed up.

It was a total disaster!

We ended up learning a lot.

Have you or anyone you know had any interesting travel experiences?

👁 **Look at the pictures. What is each person doing? How do you think they feel?**

🎧 CD 2, Tracks 45–48

First Listening:
What is the point of each travel story?

1. ⬜ When you travel, it's exciting to try new things.
   ⬜ When you travel, it's important to learn about the place you're going to.

2. ⬜ In some cultures, people are very generous to strangers.
   ⬜ In some cultures, people are suspicious of strangers.

3. ⬜ People in different cultures have different ideas about danger.
   ⬜ In some countries, the roads are not very developed.

🎧 CD 2, Tracks 45–48

Second Listening:
How did it all turn out?

1. ⬜ She left before she got to the top.
   ⬜ She went back to get more warm clothes.

2. ⬜ He stayed at the train station.
   ⬜ He stayed at the stranger's house.

3. ⬜ The bus crashed.
   ⬜ The bus continued on to Kathmandu.

PREPARE

 Randy is in a travel agency in Thailand. Why do you think he has ketchup all over his shirt?

- ☐ His friend accidentally squirted it on him.
- ☐ He got into an argument with the travel agent.
- ☐ He was trying to make the other tourists laugh.
- ☐ He wanted to get a memorable photo.
- ☐ Something else? _____

Now listen and check.

CD 2, Tracks 49–50

GET THE MAIN IDEAS

Listen again. Put these events in order. (1–10.)

CD 2, Tracks 49–50

___ A van pulls up.

___ They arrive at the bus terminal.

___ Tim and Randy go to the travel agency.

___ Tim and Randy don't get on the van.

___ Tim and Randy get on the van.

___ Randy demands a taxi ride.

___ The woman squirts ketchup on Randy.

___ Randy gets angry at the travel agent.

___ Randy regrets his behavior.

___ The van pulls up again.

RESPOND TO THE IDEAS

1. **What do you think caused the misunderstanding between Randy and the travel agent?**
2. **Have you had a travel experience that you regretted or that you learned something from?**

BAD TRIP

1. Create a terrible trip. Include as many details as possible. You can use the phrases below.

Last year we went to _____

The weather was _____

Our tour guide was _____

He told us to _____

Our hotel was _____

For dinner, we ate _____

It was terrible, but at least we _____

2. Form groups. Tell your group about your trip.

3. Have the member from each group with the worst trip tell the class about it.

"*You can make some real money.*"

Warm Up

 Read this magazine article about smart investing. Write the missing words and phrases.

get-rich-quick	gullible	stock market
broker	real estate	start (your) own
risky	invest	set up
come up with		

SAFE INVESTING

Here are some guidelines for safe investing:

1. There are plenty of people out there offering to teach you ways of earning money. Beware of _____ schemes. These are programs that falsely promise big money with little effort. Remember, if it sounds too good to be true, it probably is!

2. Research any money-making opportunity carefully before you hand over your cash. Some companies make a lot of money off of people who are so _____ they will trust anyone.

3. Putting your money into any opportunity is _____, so make sure you don't invest more money than you can afford to lose.

4. Now, if you're ready to _____, check out these ways:

5. _____: Buying and selling homes and other kinds of property can be a good money-maker for some people.

6. The _____: Buying and selling shares in a successful company could make you big bucks. Just be careful to hire a good _____, someone who has a lot of knowledge of the market.

7. Internet Business: Many people these days are _____ing their _____ business on the Web. You may want to consider taking some classes to learn how to successfully _____ your new business.

8. Remember, these opportunities are not for everyone. Select the one that's right for you or _____ your own ideas to make money!

 Now listen and check.

CD 2, Track 51

Think of a good way to make money. Suggest it to your partner.

USEFUL EXPRESSIONS
It's worth a try.
Let's put our money into ...
Some people make a lot off ...
We could invest in ...
I hope I get that lucky.

Listening Task

 Look at the pictures. What is each person's investment idea?

 First Listening: What is each person doing to try to make money?

CD 2,
Tracks 52–56

 Second Listening: What does the other person think of the plan?

CD 2, Tracks 52–56

1.
   ☐ Buying and selling stocks is really fun.
   ☐ The plan might fail and she could lose a lot of money.

2.
   ☐ It's not a good idea because some-body else already thought of it.
   ☐ Starting a new company is too difficult.

3.
   ☐ He won't make much money.
   ☐ He might get lucky like other people who have sold old collector's items.

4.
   ☐ Nobody will use the product.
   ☐ Nobody needs the product.

PREPARE

 You are going to listen to a TV infomercial for a product called *Real Money*. What do you think it will be about?

- ☐ real estate investments
- ☐ investing in the stock market
- ☐ starting your own company
- ☐ making money at home
- ☐ some other idea? _____

What kind of person do you think Steven Crowe is?

- ☐ honest
- ☐ funny
- ☐ dishonest
- ☐ intelligent

🎧 **Now listen and check.**

CD 2, Tracks 57–58

GET THE MAIN IDEAS

🎧 **What information does the infomercial include?**

CD 2, Tracks 57–58

- ☐ a plan for investing in real estate
- ☐ a plan for investing in the stock market
- ☐ comments from people who have made a lot of money
- ☐ promises that you will get rich
- ☐ the price of the product
- ☐ an address where you can send money
- ☐ something else? _____

RESPOND TO THE IDEAS

1. **What do you think of Steven Crowe's ideas for investing in real estate? Do you think it would be easy to make money this way? Why or why not?**

2. **Do you think it's possible to get rich quick? What are the best ways to make money?**

INFOMERCIAL

1. Form groups of three or four. Make a one-minute infomercial to promote an investment idea. (Look at the box below to help you choose your investment idea.) Divide your infomercial into four parts:
   1. 15 seconds to introduce the idea
   2. 15 seconds to introduce the company's founder
   3. 15 seconds for testimonials from satisfied customers
   4. 15 seconds to tell viewers how to sign up and how much it will cost them

Real estate	Gold
Stock market	Antiques
Internet start-up	Agriculture
Oil	

2. Present your infomercial to the class. As a class, vote on the best infomercial.

"She's still in our hearts."

Warm Up

 Read this magazine article about dealing with different types of loss. Write the missing words and phrases.

struggle	look up	go through	spouse
eventually	manage	focus	
cheerful	read your mind	homesickness	

DEALING WITH LOSS

1. **W**e all recognize the most serious kinds of loss: A husband who loses his _____ may experience a deep sense of grief. A person living abroad may deal with __struggle__. But seemingly less serious types of loss, such as changing jobs, can also create some of the same strong feelings. The good news is that _____ing __through__ any type of loss helps us to learn and grow.

So how can you deal with loss and what can you do for your loved ones when they are _____ing with grief?

Here are some tips:

2. **Dealing with your own loss:**

- You cannot _____ successfully on your own. You need family and friends.

- Remember, your friends can't _____ _____. You must talk to them.

 Now listen and check.

CD 2, Track 59

- You don't need to put on a smile or keep up a _____ face. Grief is not a sign of weakness. It is the result of a strong relationship and deserves the honor of strong emotion.

- _____ing on your loss will not help you hold on to memories. When a person moves on and makes a new life, positive memories return more clearly.

3. **Helping friends and family:**

- Be patient. _____ your friend will recover. But healing takes time.

- Be prepared for setbacks. Even when things start to _____ and life seems happier, depression can still return. Let your friend know you will always be there.

USEFUL EXPRESSIONS
It takes time.
Sometimes it's for the best.
Give it some time.
You can't do it on your own.
You have to hang in there.

 Which of the above ideas do you agree with? Which do you disagree with?

72

Look at the pictures. What has happened in each person's life?

 First Listening: What loss has each person experienced?

2, Tracks 60–64

Second Listening: How does the other person respond?
(There may be more than one answer.)

CD 2, Tracks 60–64

1.
   - [ ] She listens to his memories.
   - [ ] She suggests that he get a new dog.
   - [ ] She agrees that Champ was a wonderful pet.

2.
   - [ ] She talks about her own experience.
   - [ ] She encourages Theresa to express her feelings.
   - [ ] She agrees that divorce is a difficult loss.

3.
   - [ ] He tells Joe he was too good for Gwen.
   - [ ] He tells Joe the breakup was the right thing to do.
   - [ ] He tells Joe he'll find another girlfriend soon.

4.
   - [ ] He tells Sung-Hee that she'll feel better soon.
   - [ ] He tells Sung-Hee to cook some Korean food to ease her homesickness.
   - [ ] He helps Sung-Hee find a friend from her native culture.

PREPARE

Clayton Hayes is a guest on *Life's Concerns.* He's going to tell talk-show host Whitney Opal about losing his wife. What do you think he might talk about?

- ☐ how they first met
- ☐ how long they were together
- ☐ how he manages without her
- ☐ how she died
- ☐ good memories
- ☐ how he feels now

Now listen and check.

CD 2, Tracks 65–66

GET THE MAIN IDEAS

How does Clayton feel about his late wife? You can check more than one sentence.

CD 2, Tracks 65–66

- ☐ He's angry that she's gone and is hoping to find someone new.
- ☐ He's sad that she's gone but also appreciates his memories of her.
- ☐ He's upset that she died without understanding how much he loved her.
- ☐ He misses her but is glad that her pain is over.

RESPOND TO THE IDEAS

1. **What advice would you give to Clayton Hayes?**
2. **It is difficult to know how to respond to someone who has experienced a loss. What are some ways to help someone who has lost a close friend or family member? Which ways are helpful? Which are not helpful?**

WHO WOULD YOU BRING BACK?

If you could bring one famous person from history back to life, who would it be?

1. Make groups of three or four. Brainstorm five or six people from history you would like to bring back.

2. Of these five or six people, discuss who would be the three best people to bring back, and why. Your group has to agree on who they would be.

3. Of these three people, decide who would be the one best person to bring back, and why. Your group has to agree on who it would be.

4. Share your results with the whole class. Who did each group choose?

OPTIONS

1. What questions would you ask this person? Each group member can ask one or two questions. How do you think the person would answer each question?

2. What do you think this person would do if they were alive today?

3. Each person in the group tells about someone you knew personally and would like to bring back to life. Tell what was great about this person, and why this person was special to you.

PART 1. Hearing the correct words.

Listen and write the missing words.

CD 2, Track 67

1. You should have seen the _____ look on the accounting manager's face when he saw my pink shirt with the purple necktie.

2. Today was so busy that I never left my _____ all afternoon!

3. Don't get so _____ about a little mistake. Everyone makes mistakes at some time in their career.

4. I'm _____ reducing the amount of time I spend on video games.

5. I wonder if I'm _____ to chocolate. Do you think that's possible?

6. My dentist said I really have to _____ the amount of soda I drink.

7. I slipped and fell in the pool, and my new suit was completely _____.

8. The shopkeeper said she didn't want to lose money, but I was _____ about the price I was willing to pay.

9. Because we missed the overnight bus by five minutes, we were _____ in the countryside for two more days!

10. If I were you, I wouldn't invest my money in that company. It sounds like a _____ to me.

11. This is our chance to _____ in a hurry!

12. If you look or act _____, I promise you that someone will cheat you out of your money.

13. Having a busy job can help you when you're _____ a difficult time.

14. When her parents separated, she didn't think things would ever _____.

15. When you _____ with the pain of losing a loved one, you realize how precious every day is.

PART 2. Understanding conversations.

Listen to each conversation. Then circle the answers.

CD 2, Tracks 68–77

1. Who is Nancy?
   (a) The company president
   (b) The cook in the cafeteria
   (c) The supervisor
   (d) The secretary

2. Why does the speaker disapprove of Elizabeth's behavior?
   (a) She does sloppy work.
   (b) She comes to work late.
   (c) She dresses too casually.
   (d) She dresses too formally.

3. How did Carrie find out about Mark and Sarah breaking up?
   (a) Sarah called her to tell her.
   (b) She was eavesdropping.
   (c) Sarah came to her apartment to tell her.
   (d) Dennis told her.

4. Why are the women upset with the man?
   (a) He's using his cell phone in a restaurant.
   (b) He's lying to his friend.
   (c) He's ignoring them.
   (d) He's sitting at their table.

5. Why did the guide call the woman "Loca"?
   (a) Because she was crazy.
   (b) Because she was German.
   (c) Because she didn't bring a bag.
   (d) Because she was the first woman to hike on the mountain.

6. Why did the traveler stay with Yuri?

    (a) Because he couldn't find a hotel room.

    (b) Because he and Yuri were old friends.

    (c) Because he and Yuri were related.

    (d) Because Yuri had a big house.

7. Why doesn't the friend think it's a good idea to buy and sell stocks online?

    (a) You need a broker.

    (b) You need a lot of money.

    (c) It sounds too risky.

    (d) She's done it before and it failed.

8. Which is true about the man selling his comic books?

    (a) He's going to sell them to children.

    (b) He bought them when he was a kid.

    (c) He stole them when he was a kid.

    (d) He hopes to get a dollar for each comic book.

9. What was Diego's dog's name?

    (a) Champ

    (b) Chimp

    (c) Chap

    (d) Sam

10. What does Sung-Hee miss?

    (a) Her boyfriend

    (b) New Year's parties

    (c) Her mother's cooking

    (d) Her Korean neighbor

🎧 **Listen to the conversation. Write the missing words.**

Self-Study CD, Track 2

Charisse: Karen, I can't get over how gorgeous you look. I guess you must've _____ become _____ an actress, like you always wanted.

Karen: Thanks, but you're not going to _____ believe _____ this.

Charisse: What?

Karen: Well, I moved away to Hollywood and did the _____ waitress thing for a while.

Charisse: Yeah?

Karen: Eventually, I got a small part in a horror movie, and that's when I _____ my true calling.

Charisse: What's that? Playing zombies?

Karen: Nope. I've become a movie makeup artist!

Charisse: No way! That's so amazing! But what made you _____ up acting?

Karen: I guess I just _____ working behind the scenes. But enough about me. How are you and Craig?

Charisse: Craig? Oh, him. You know, we _____ up about a year after you left town.

Karen: Oh, I'm sorry. It just seemed like you two were so _____ to get married and start a family.

Charisse: Funny how that _____ up. I was too busy with school and then my job, and we just sort of drifted apart.

Karen: Huh! So what've you been doing all this time, Charisse?

Charisse: Well, a few years ago I got a great job with an advertising agency. And guess what?

Karen: What?

Charisse: They've just _____ me. I'm an account executive now!

Karen: Wow, pretty impressive.

BONUS QUESTION

Imagine you are Karen or Charisse. Write a journal entry describing your meeting with your old friend.

Listen to the conversation. Write the missing words.

Study CD, Track 4

Cesar: TJ, my man! How's it goin'?

TJ: Hey, Cesar. What's up, dude?

Cesar: Oh, not much. But you, man. You're all over the place. I saw you on TV last week. The Pro-Am skateboarding championship. Man, you tore it up on the half-pipe.

TJ: I guess I did OK. I got second place.

Cesar: That flip you did was totally _____. Anyway, I can't believe you've gone pro, man. You've totally made it.

TJ: Yeah, I know. Contests, _____, kids asking for my autograph all the time. It's weird.

Cesar: Sounds like it. But good weird.

TJ: Yeah. And you won't even _____ what the latest is.

Cesar: What?

TJ: Nike wants me to do a commercial. They've been calling my _____. Nike, man.

Cesar: Wow! I don't believe that. That's crazy, man. You've got it made.

TJ: Yeah, sorta.

Cesar: What's wrong?

TJ: Well, you know the fame and _____ are great, but sometimes I just want to have my old life back again.

Cesar: Why? With the way things are going for you?

TJ: No, but it's my family and my friends, like you. They think I'm too good for them now. They think I don't have time for the stuff we used to do, like go to movies and just hang out.

Cesar: Wow, man. That's rough. But you know, your life is kinda different now.

TJ: Sure, I mean, people _____ me and stuff, but I'm still the same person I was before I went pro. I just wish everyone would understand that.

Cesar: Don't you like all the _____ you're getting?

TJ: I dunno, man. The truth is, it's kind of _____. I guess I'm shy or something.

Cesar: You? No way, TJ. I thought you lived for the crowds.

TJ: Nah, it's the sport I love. I can live without the _____.

Cesar: So what are you gonna do, man?

TJ: Just keep doing what I'm doing. I've gotta be true to myself, no _____ what anyone else thinks about it.

BONUS QUESTION

TJ's agent tells him to move to a different city, and away from his friends and family, for his skateboarding career. Write the conversation.

Unit 3 Self-Study

Listen to the conversations. Write the missing words.

Self-Study CD Track 6

Part 1

Andrea: Andrea Price on *Who Needs Advice*. What's your problem?

Jackie: Hi, I'm Jackie, from Toronto.

Andrea: Jackie, what's your _____?

Jackie: My parents are driving me crazy! I'm in college, and my parents make me come home before midnight. Plus …

Andrea: Just a second, Jackie. Slow down. You're in college, you're living at _____, your parents want you home at midnight. What's wrong with that?

Jackie: Well, it's not only that. They always want to know who I'm going out with, and if I've done my homework. How can I get them to leave me alone?

Andrea: Jackie, _____ up already. If you live at home, you should _____ their rules or move out of the house. Clear enough?

Part 2

Andrea: Andrea Price on *Who Needs Advice*.

Beatrice: This is Beatrice from Atlanta.

Andrea: OK, Beatrice. What's your problem?

Beatrice: I need some advice about dieting. Every time I go on a diet, I _____ a few pounds, but it only lasts a little while.

Andrea: Uh huh. Go on.

Beatrice: Once I start eating normally again, I always _____ the weight back.

Andrea: Do you _____ regularly?

Beatrice: No.

Andrea: There's your problem. You can't lose weight without exercise. Talk to your doctor about an exercise _____, and stick to it.

Part 3

Andrea: Andrea Price on *Who Needs Advice*.

Pete: This is Pete, from Denver.

Andrea: What's your problem?

Pete: Could I ask you something?

Andrea: That's what I'm here for.

Pete: Well, my car has been making funny _____ lately. Like this—fffft fffft fffft fffft—but only when it's moving. When it's _____, it makes sounds sort of like, vvvttt, vvvtttt, vvvttt.

Andrea: Look, Pete.

Pete: I really don't know what to do.

Andrea: Look, Pete, I give advice about _____, not cars. You need to call a _____.

BONUS QUESTION

What kind of problem would you ask Andrea for advice about? Write the conversation.

Listen to the conversation. Write the missing words.

Study CD, Track 8

Lydia: OK, Greg, I got the wedding invitations back from the printers. Let's do this!

Greg: OK, I'm ready.

Lydia: Got your list?

Greg: Yeah, I just have a short list, though. Just my parents, and my brother Tim and his wife, and my sister Tanya, and Jamie, my old friend from college, and that's about it. I can't think of anyone else that I really want to invite.

Lydia: Greg, that's like, what, ten people? Are you joking? This is our wedding.

Greg: Well, I guess we could invite my mom's _____ Abigail. She lives nearby, but I don't know her very well. She's kind of crazy. She has, like, fifteen cats.

Lydia: Greg, if she's _____, you should invite her.

Greg: I guess.

Lydia: So, including your mom's cousin Abigail, you've now got a grand total of eleven _____. That just isn't enough to fill up a reception room.

Greg: Well, how many people are you inviting?

Lydia: Um, let's see. Here's my list. I've got my brother and his wife.

Greg: Right.

Lydia: And her parents and _____.

Greg: You're inviting your sister-in-law's relatives, too?

Lydia: Greg, this is a family _____. Can't leave anyone out.

Greg: Can't leave anyone out?

Lydia: And then there's my mother's two brothers and their families.

Greg: They'll come all the way from San Francisco for this?

Lydia: Oh, absolutely. And then my aunt Chia-Lin.

Greg: I thought she lived in Shanghai.

Lydia: She does, but she'll come for the wedding.

Greg: Really?

Lydia: She wouldn't miss it for the world, and besides, my mother would never _____ her if she didn't come to my wedding.

Greg: Ah.

Lydia: And then my father will want to invite all his _____ friends from work.

Greg: Wait a sec. Your father's friends from work are coming? How many is that?

Lydia: Oh, Greg, he's in the restaurant business. He's got so many friends. There must be like, one, two, three, eight people who work in the restaurant alone, and then the suppliers, and all of his regular big _____. Maybe eighty or ninety. Something like that.

Greg: Eighty people!

Lydia: There's no way he wouldn't invite all of them to his daughter's wedding. It'd be an insult!

Greg: But I thought we were just inviting family and _____ friends.

Lydia: Believe me, my father's business associates are like family.

Greg: Wow! How many people are on that list there?

Lydia: Oh, just a few. This is just like three or four hundred people. I'm trying to keep it _____.

Greg: Gosh, Lydia, where are we going to have this wedding, in Yankee Stadium?

BONUS QUESTION

Imagine that you're planning a wedding with your soon-to-be spouse. Write the conversation.

Listen to the lecture. Write the missing words.

Self-Study CD, Track 10

Our topic today is decision making. We make decisions every day, right? Maybe about simple, _____ things like which train to take to work or should you get a puppy as a pet, and also more _____ things like what to major in at college or whether to take a job offer in a new city.

We're going to look at four dimensions of the decision making process, OK? Approach, information, risk, and decisiveness.

The first dimension is approach, or the way that you view the decision-making process. There are two types of decision makers here: originators and adapters. Adapters tend to think in terms of the _____ change necessary to produce the results they want. They stick with ideas that have worked in the past. Originators, on the other hand, tend to produce decisions that are less _____ to past ideas. They make decisions that seem unique and creative.

The second dimension is information. What kind of information do you need to make a decision? Are you a concrete information processor or an abstract information processor? Concrete information processors need _____ and detailed information before making a decision. They prefer to work with clear, absolute, and exact facts and values. Abstract information processors, on the other hand, focus on the big picture and _____ information before they make their decision.

The third dimension is risk. What kind of risk taker are you when you make a big decision? How do you deal with struggles and challenges when you face a _____ decision? Two types of risk takers here: conciliators and challengers. Conciliators prefer to be cautious and avoid risks. They avoid taking actions that might involve losing too much. The other type is the challenger. And a challenger will take a more _____ and risky choice in order to get a greater gain, even if the situation has a good chance of turning out badly.

The fourth dimension is decisiveness—how fast you make the decision, and how quickly you take steps towards implementing your decision. For this dimension, the two types of decision makers are called organized and flexible. Organized decision makers are quick to choose—bang, come on, make a decision—and also quick to act upon their decisions: OK, let's do it! They commit their _____ and time sooner than others. Flexible decision makers, on the other hand, are slow to choose and also slow to act upon their decisions. They tend to change plans frequently, and they also _____ or postpone their plans unless they become absolutely necessary.

So that's the theory: four dimensions of decision making. Where do you stand in each dimension? There's no right or wrong way to make a decision, but by understanding our own decision-making styles, we can make more effective, well-informed, and conscious decisions.

BONUS QUESTION
Think of a time when you made a big decision in your life. What kind of decision-making strategy did you use? Write about it.

🎧 **Listen to the conversations. Write the missing words.**

:udy CD, Track 12

Part 1

Jennifer: Tell me how your _____ and _____ have prepared you to be a manager in our travel company.

Sumi: Well, as my resume shows, I have a bachelor's degree in travel industry management from an American university, and I worked for five years in one of the top travel companies in Japan. After two years I was promoted to a _____ position that was very similar to the job you are offering here.

Jennifer: I see. So you have supervised people in your previous _____?

Sumi: Yes. Actually, I supervised a staff of about twenty people.

Part 2

Sumi: Hello?

Jennifer: I'm calling for Sumi Wilson.

Sumi: This is Sumi.

Jennifer: Hi! This is Jennifer Bates of World Trek travel agency. I'm calling with what I _____ will be good news.

Sumi: Yes?

Jennifer: We'd like to offer you a position as a customer service _____.

Sumi: Sorry, but did you just say customer service? I was applying for the management position.

Jennifer: Yes, I know. Actually, we've _____ someone else for the management position, but we really liked you, so we'd like to hire you in customer service.

Sumi: I see. Well, since I was _____ to get the management position, I think I'll need to think about this. Could I call you back tomorrow?

Part 3

Rick: Hello?

Sumi: It's me. World Trek called.

Rick: So, did you get the job?

Sumi: No, but they offered me a job as a customer service representative, selling and leading tours to various places in Asia.

Rick: That's not fair! You were _____ for the management job!

Sumi: That's what I thought, too. But I _____ think they were worried about my English. I'm sure they want a native speaker to be the manager.

Rick: But that's ridiculous! Your English is great. You know, if that's their _____, I'm glad you're not going to be working there.

Sumi: Actually, I've been thinking about it a lot, and I really want to _____ the job as a customer service rep.

Rick: What? Why?

Sumi: Well, it's a good chance to show them how much I know, what I can do. And they can see for themselves how good my English is, too! Then, whenever the next management position comes up, they'll know I'm the perfect choice!

Rick: Well, in that case, go for it! And let's go out for dinner tonight to celebrate!

BONUS QUESTION
What do you think about Sumi's situation. Write your opinion.

🎧 **Listen to the conversations. Write the missing words.**

Self-Study CD, Track 14

Part 1

Amy: I know I have a picture of Luis around here somewhere. Oh, here it is.

Becky: Wow, he's so _____! He looks like a Greek statue.

Amy: Yeah, he is very _____. But I didn't think so when I first met him.

Becky: You didn't?

Amy: No. You know what I noticed when I first met him? He has really hairy hands.

Becky: What?

Amy: Yeah. His hands are just really hairy. Plus, his clothes were way more _____ than I usually like. He just wasn't my type. And on top of all of that, he was _____ than me.

Becky: So how come you went out with him?

Amy: Well, he was just really sweet and funny, and I was so _____ just hanging out with him. And the first time we went out he just swept me away with his _____.

Becky: Really? How?

Amy: He was just really easy to talk to.

Becky: But still, if all those things bothered you, about his hands and all.

Amy: Well, you know, none of that was important once I got to know him more. His personality and the way we got along just made it clear to me that he is "the one."

Becky: So, when's the big day?

Part 2

Bob: Luis, I'm so happy for you and Amy.

Luis: Thanks. She's a great girl. And she's perfect for me. We just "_____," you know?

Bob: So then I guess you just always knew she was the person for you?

Luis: Well, not exactly.

Bob: It wasn't love at first _____?

Luis: No. But don't tell Amy that. She's such a _____. She'd probably like it if I said I fell for her immediately.

Bob: But you didn't?

Luis: No. It took me a while to warm up to Amy. She just wasn't my type.

Bob: Really? Why? Didn't you think she was attractive?

Luis: Well, she was so thin and _____. I usually like a girl with a few _____.

Bob: Then what made you decide to ask her out?

Luis: I didn't. She asked me out!

Bob: She did? And how did you feel about that?

Luis: I wasn't sure at first. But you know, I ended up really liking that part of her personality. She's _____ and she goes after what she wants. And once I started looking at her more, I really liked her physically.

Bob: Well, you two sure make a great couple!

BONUS QUESTION

Think of someone you like. What good qualities do you like? What bad qualities do you overlook or not notice anymore?

🎧 **Listen to the conversation. Write the missing words.**
Study CD, Track 16

Greg: Hello, this is *Tech Trek*, and I'm your host, Greg McFee. Today we're going to review three new video games that everyone's talking about. First, there's "The Butcher." The player is an undercover cop who used to be a butcher. Imagine that. Super _____, super fast game. Next is "Pirate Party," which is based on last summer's hit movie about a band of pirates that attacks cruise ships and beach resorts. Last is "Marooned on Mars," a video game that takes place in 2250 in an _____ colony on Mars. The object of the game is to construct a spaceship to get back to Earth. OK, before we get to the reviews, we have a special guest on *Tech Trek*—Jeff Townsend, developer of "The Butcher." Jeff, thanks for coming in today.

Jeff: My pleasure, Greg.

Greg: So, Jeff. "The Butcher." A lot of people are talking about your game, and most of them are saying that it might be too violent.

Jeff: Well, it is violent. I mean, it's about a cop, who was once a butcher, who hunts down criminals and chops them up into steaks. There's a lot of _____, a lot of body parts.

Greg: Right. I've played the game. There is a lot of blood, and some people have a problem with that. A lot of people think that video games like "The Butcher" actually cause violence, that they're a bad _____ on children.

Jeff: Yeah, I hear that a lot. But I don't know. To me, video games are just _____. I think people can tell the difference between a video game and real life.

Greg: Even kids?

Jeff: Even kids. I don't think anyone is going to play "The Butcher" and then go out and make criminals into _____. You're not going to become more violent if you play "The Butcher."

Greg: Maybe so, but …

Jeff: In fact, I was reading the newspaper, and there are some _____ who think that playing violent video games can actually make you less violent.

Greg: Hmm. That's interesting.

Jeff: Yeah, they say if you get all your anger and _____ out in a video game, you'll be a lot more relaxed in your regular life.

Greg: So if you were a really angry person, it might be a good idea to play "The Butcher," right? You could hack up criminals for an hour and then go on with the rest of your day in a _____, happy mood.

Jeff: Exactly. Playing a video game might be better than _____ or seeing a psychiatrist, or anything like that.

Greg: But what about this, Jeff? Some people say video games can become an _____. Some kids play for hours every day. Are video games addictive?

Jeff: Well, it's definitely hard not to play "The Butcher" all the time. It's so _____.

Greg: That it is. Anyway, thanks for joining us on *Tech Trek*, Jeff.

Jeff: Any time.

BONUS QUESTION

What would you talk about with Jeff Townsend if you were the host of a show like *Tech Trek*? Write the conversation.

Listen to the conversation. Write the missing words.

Self-Study CD, Track 18

Kara: Steve, remember the older _____ that I rent my apartment from?

Steve: Yeah?

Kara: Well, the woman has been coming up to see how I'm doing. At first I was really _____ you know. It's nice to feel that people are concerned when you live alone.

Steve: Yeah, it is nice.

Kara: Now, though, she comes every day, sometimes more than once! She always brings me homemade soup.

Steve: Homemade soup! That is so great! I wish someone cooked for me.

Kara: Well, sure, having some home-cooked food is a _____, but she sits and watches me to make _____ I eat it! Last time, I had just eaten dinner when she came over and _____ that I finish a whole bowl. She wouldn't leave until I did!

Steve: Oh, c'mon. You could have it much worse.

Kara: And every time I go out she _____ out the door to ask where I'm going. It's like I'm _____ again!

Steve: Would you rather have loud neighbors who kept you up all night?

Kara: Well, it's not only her. It's the old man, too. He's such a _____, and I've always thought it was _____. You know, an old man, eighty years old, still flirting.

Steve: Uh huh.

Kara: So, today when I got home, he came up to me, gave me a _____.

Steve: Yeah, so what?

Kara: And then, he kissed me on the cheek!

Steve: Oh, no. Well, maybe you remind him of his _____.

Kara: Well, yeah, but don't you think it's kind of _____ for him to kiss me?

BONUS QUESTION

Imagine you are Kara. Write a letter to a friend or family member asking for advice. Then write a letter in response to Kara's problem.

Listen to Petra Nemcova's story. Write the missing words.

tudy CD, Track 20

I opened my eyes and looked down. Black, filthy water _____ the lower half of my body. I couldn't even see my legs. My arms, bare, scratched, _____, and aching, were wrapped around a palm tree. I was holding on, leaning against the trunk. Black, oil-slicked, muddied water choked with debris was everywhere. I looked up. The sky was blue, clear, _____. The sun was shining. Where was I? Where was Simon? What had happened?

I remembered. Simon and I were in the bungalow when a rush of water rose up so suddenly there was not even a second to think, a rush of water that came from all directions, _____ us out into the _____ current. For one split second, before the water separated us, I saw Simon's face. "Petra!" he screamed. "Petra! What's happening?"

I couldn't answer. I didn't know. Then I lost sight of him. Seconds later, I saw him again, whirling in the _____ waters. He was a few yards ahead of me. Behind him a rooftop was sticking out of the water.

"Catch the roof! Catch the roof!" I shouted. Then he was gone. I don't know whether he heard me or not. I prayed that he would catch hold. I was sure he would. He was a strong swimmer. He had to be OK.

It was impossible to tell in which direction the waters were _____. I needed to grab onto something or be swept away. I saw another rooftop. I reached out my arms, and sending out every bit of energy I had, I grabbed the edges and held on. Instantly, my legs were _____ underneath, and everything accumulated by the raging water, the wood and metal objects, all the trash, began _____ against my hips and legs. I hung on, screaming with pain and fear. I would be crushed into nothing. For the first time, I thought of _____.

_____, the pressure of the water began to lessen. I pulled myself up onto the roof. My clothes had been torn from my body. I was naked. Then, as quickly as the first, another _____ wave rose up and poured over the rooftop. I lost my grip and was drawn down beneath the water. Frantically, I flailed my arms, trying to get out from under the thick layer of filth between me and the surface. Desperately, I fought to get some air until I had no breath left. I stopped fighting, stopped struggling, and began swallowing the inky water. A great feeling of peacefulness came over me. I surrendered to the calmness. Whatever was meant to be, whatever God will decide, it's OK.

At that moment, without any effort on my part, I was thrust through the barrier of debris to the surface. I threw my head back and gasped for air. Above me was the blue, blue sky. I was never so happy in my life to see the sky.

BONUS QUESTION

Petra was eventually rescued. What do you think she said to the people who rescued her? Write the conversation.

Unit 11 Self-Study

🎧 **Listen to the conversations. Write the missing words.**

Self-Study CD, Track 22

Part 1

Jay: Hey, Steve. How's it going? How's the new job in the promotions department?

Steve: I don't know, man. Sometimes I can't believe these people.

Jay: What do you mean? I thought you loved it here.

Steve: Yeah, I don't know. The work is good. I love promotions work. But, man, the _____ here is driving me nuts. They have so many _____!

Jay: Yeah, they kind of do. But it's just different, you know? You'll get used to it. I promise.

Steve: Really? Well, different is fine, but sometimes I think I'm going to snap. They're so _____, especially my boss.

Jay: Mr. Takahashi?

Steve: Yeah, I mean, he's a really good boss, very smart about _____, but he never really tells me what he's thinking.

Jay: Sometimes bosses are quiet like that.

Steve: But I can feel his eyes, man. It's like he's watching me all the time. I have to be at work right on time, not a second late.

Jay: Yeah. Being on time is really important here.

Steve: And meeting people is so _____. That drives me nuts. I never know what to do. Should I bow? Should I shake hands? Should I shake hands and bow at the same time? Should I say *shitsurei-shimasu*?

Jay: Actually, that might help if you learn a little Japanese.

Steve: It just seems that everyone is too _____ all the time. Can't they just relax a little bit? Everyone here is so uptight. They all sort of run around and bow and shrink whenever Takahashi comes into the office.

Jay: Well, they just have different ways of doing things, I guess. And I think they'll relax after you get to know them a bit.

Part 2

Alan: Takahashi-*san*, how is the new person in the promotions department doing?

Takahashi: You mean, Steve-*san*?

Alan: Yeah, Steve Jones. How's he doing? Is he _____ to the company working style OK?

Takahashi: Mm. *So desu-ne.*

Alan: So, still on a _____ curve?

Takahashi: Mm. He's very talented, very intelligent. And good spirit. But I think his behavior is still a little, hmm, a little difficult.

Alan: Hmm. Well, what does he do?

Takahashi: I think perhaps he doesn't understand _____ very well. Sometimes he doesn't even wear a tie.

Alan: Hmm. Maybe he thinks the promotions department should be more _____?

Takahashi: Perhaps, perhaps, hmm.

Alan: Well, how is he ... how is he about working hours?

Takahashi: Ah, this is a little problem.

Alan: Comes in late, huh?

Takahashi: Well, perhaps he doesn't understand our working system. He usually comes in around 10 o'clock. Everyone is already at their desks, working.

Alan: Mm. Well, does he get along with the other staff _____?

Takahashi: Ah. Interesting. He does, actually, so I don't want to interfere too much. They seem to like him and _____ his ideas.

Alan: Which is good.

Takahashi: Yes, that's good.

Alan: Does he deal with clients well?

Takahashi: Mm. Clients *da-ne*. This is a problem. He's improving, but ...

Alan: What do you mean? What does he do?

Takahashi: Yesterday, we had a meeting with an important client. And I introduced Steve-*san*, and he didn't bow. He just stuck out his hand and said, "Hey, nice to meet you." And I think the clients were a little embarrassed.

Alan: Which is not good.

Takahashi: No, that's not good. Mm. *Komarimashita-ne.*

Alan: But he may improve.

Takahashi: Yes, yes. He may improve. I hope.

BONUS QUESTION

What is one thing in your culture that visitors have trouble understanding? Why? How do they react?

Unit 12 Self-Study

🎧 **Listen to the conversations. Write the missing words.**

Study CD, Track 24

Part 1

Dr. Morrissey: Well, Mr. Garcia, your test results are in. You've got high cholesterol and a bit of a weight problem. I think we need to discuss some serious _____ changes.

Mr. Garcia: All right, Doctor, I'm ready. Go ahead and scold me.

Dr. Morrissey: Oh, I'm not here to scold you, Mr. Garcia, just encourage you.

Mr. Garcia: That's a relief!

Dr. Morrissey: But I would suggest making some _____ changes in your diet. For example, cutting down on the amount of fatty foods you eat.

Mr. Garcia: It's going to be tough to change my diet. I think I'm _____ to fast food!

Dr. Morrissey: Yes, well, unfortunately, you're going to have to. And it's more than just your diet you need to _____. I also want you to start exercising. Exercise is going to keep your heart healthy and help you lose some of those unwanted pounds.

Mr. Garcia: Oh, no! I just knew you were going to tell me that! I can't stand exercising. It's so boring!

Dr. Morrissey: Oh, I'm sure you can find some physical activity you enjoy. Now, about your stress _____ at work.

Mr. Garcia: You can't just take a break when you're the CEO of an international company, you know! And even when I do get a day off from work, I've got three teenagers at home to keep me stressed out.

Dr. Morrissey: Hmm. Well, you're going to have to find some time somewhere in your schedule for _____. Your health depends on it.

Mr. Garcia: OK. I think I get the message. I'll do my best, but you know what they say, Doctor: Old habits die hard.

Part 2

Sandra: David, is that you? I hardly even _____ you!

Mr. Garcia: Yeah, it's the new and _____ me!

Sandra: Wow! You must have lost some weight.

Mr. Garcia: Yeah, like fifty pounds.

Sandra: What have you been up to?

Mr. Garcia: Well, for starters, I _____ my junk food habit. No more fast food.

Sandra: You're kidding! I thought you were addicted to those Big Macs!

Mr. Garcia: I was, but not anymore. It's salads for lunch now. I've also started taking a ballroom dance class with my wife. It's a fun way to keep my weight under _____, and my wife and I get to spend more time together.

Sandra: That's fantastic! And how's Fiberglass International?

Mr. Garcia: Pretty good! I recently took a little _____ from work, and you know, the strangest thing happened! When I returned from my vacation, I found that I had a lot more _____ at work. I think I'm going to go to Hawaii next month.

Sandra: Well, that's just wonderful. Keep up the good work!

BONUS QUESTION
Imagine you are Mr. Garcia's doctor. What advice would you give him about his habits?

Unit 13 Self-Study

🎧 **Listen to the conversation. Write the missing words.**

Self-Study CD, Track 26

Sue: Randy, what's going on in this picture? It looks like you have blood all over your shirt.

Randy: Oh, no, that's not blood. It's ketchup.

Sue: Ketchup? What happened?

Randy: This happened when Tim and I were _____ around Asia. We were in Bangkok.

Sue: Yeah.

Randy: And we had reservations to catch an overnight bus to Chiang Mai.

Sue: Yeah.

Randy: And we were waiting at a kind of restaurant that was sort of a travel agency, and we went early, but the bus didn't come, and I was getting kind of _____.

Sue: Yeah, but what's that got to do with ketchup?

Randy: So, I was beginning to wonder if we'd been cheated, because we'd already paid for our tickets in _____.

Sue: Right.

Randy: Then, finally, a van _____ up, and we thought, no, this is not the bus, but then everyone else who was waiting pushed right past us and jumped in, and, bam, just like that, the van drove away. Then this sweet little Thai woman, who was the travel agent who _____ us the tickets, came up to us.

Sue: Yeah, and ...

Randy: And she said, "Why you no get on?" And Tim was like, "That wasn't the bus, was it?" "Only one. Why you not get on?" And I didn't know what she was talking about.

Sue: So what happened?

Randy: Well, the travel agent just shrugged and turned and went inside her shop. Neither of us could believe it. I started to get really angry, like we'd been _____. Now it's dark. We're _____ in this little restaurant.

Sue: Oh, no.

Randy: I followed her inside. I started _____. I told her, "We paid for the bus. You didn't tell us to look for a van. Now you have to get us a taxi to Chiang Mai. Now." I started _____ at the clock. I think that was the last straw for the woman, because she started shouting. "You no go. You no go Chiang Mai!" She grabbed a ketchup bottle off the table, you know one of those plastic squirt ketchup bottles, and she squirted ketchup at me!

Sue: No! She didn't!

Randy: Yeah! She did. And then she threw the bottle at me. And Tim snapped the picture. Just then the same van pulled up and the woman said, "Now you go."

Sue: So you got on the van?

Randy: Yeah. We ended up at the bus _____, where this big, air-conditioned _____ bus was waiting to go to Chiang Mai. And all the people who had pushed ahead of us earlier were there, waiting to leave. I felt so stupid for getting angry at the woman and making such a fool of myself.

Sue: You must have felt terrible.

Randy: Yeah, I wish there was some way I could go back and apologize to her. I realized that I have to be more _____, especially when I'm in another country.

BONUS QUESTION

Do you know a travel story like this? Write the story in the form of a conversation.

🎧 **Listen to the infomercial. Write the missing words.**

tudy CD, Track 28

Ed: Are you worried about having enough money? Are you worried about paying your _____? Well, worry no more!

Customer 1: I used to watch every penny. But now I'm worth four _____ dollars, and it's all thanks to Steven Crowe!

Customer 2: I used to get headaches from worrying about money. I had a lot of credit card _____, and my mortgage payments were killing me. Then I got Steven Crowe's videos and learned how to make real money.

Ed: *Real Money*. That's the name of this three-video set by Steven Crowe. Let Steven show you how to become _____ independent buying and selling real estate.

Steven: Hi! I'm Steven Crowe. I used to worry about money, too. I felt like a _____ of the system. But then I found a way to make the system work, for me.

Ed: What's the trick, Steven?

Steven: There's no trick, Ed. It's simple, once you understand how real _____ really works. All you need to know is how to buy low and sell _____. And that's exactly what my videos teach you to do.

Ed: And you can get really rich?

Steven: Just ask some people who have *Real Money*.

Customer 1: After I got the *Real Money* videos, I bought my first house, following Steven's simple rules. Six months later I sold it and bought two more houses. A year after that, I had enough money to quit my job. Now I have more money than I'll ever need, and it's such a great _____.

Steven: I want you to have that feeling, too. And you can.

Ed: Call now to order *Real Money*. 1-800-289-7325. That's 1-800-BUY-REAL. Only three payments of $19.95 each, plus _____ and handling. All major credit cards welcome. Get it today for a worry-free tomorrow! _____ may vary.

BONUS QUESTION
Think of a get-rich-quick product or scheme. Write an infomercial for it.

🎧 **Listen to *Life's Concerns*. Write the missing words.**

Self-Study CD, Track 30

Whitney: Welcome to *Life's Concerns*. I'm your host, Whitney Opal. Today our program is about _____ with loss. One of the hardest things in life is losing a spouse after so man years together. Mr. Clayton Hayes is here today to _____ his story. Thank you fc joining us, Mr. Hayes.

Clayton: Call me Clayton, please.

Whitney: OK, Clayton. I'd like to ask you a few questions about how you're _____. Is that OK?

Clayton: Yes, that's fine. I can talk about it.

Whitney: All right. Well, your wife _____ away two years ago. Is that correct?

Clayton: Yep. Maggie was 79, just about to turn 80 when she passed away. I never really _____ her to go. She was still too young.

Whitney: I'm sorry. Do you _____ telling us how she died?

Clayton: Cancer. She had it for about a year, but it seemed longer than that to me. And she was in so much pain at the end. Oh.

Whitney: I'm really sorry. That must have been very difficult for you.

Clayton: Yeah. At the end, there, you could tell she just wanted it to be over. She tried to keep up a _____ face for me, but you can't hide things from someone you've been married to for 56 years, you know.

Whitney: I'm sure that's true. You get to know someone pretty well in 56 years, don't you?

Clayton: Oh, you bet you do. You share so many years of your life with someone, and when they're gone, oh, there's a big _____ that no one can fill up. You just feel lonely. Very, very lonely.

Whitney: I imagine you have some wonderful _____, as well.

Clayton: Oh, yeah. We had a lot of good times, Maggie and me. Oh, boy, the stories I could tell!

Whitney: Well, Clayton, you sure do have a lot of memories from your time with Maggie to _____!

Clayton: Yeah, I sure do.

Whitney: I think it's important to remember that when we _____ someone close to us, we don't lose those memories. The _____ is still with us in that way.

BONUS QUESTION

Imagine that you're the next guest on *Life's Concerns*. What kind of loss would you talk about? Write the conversation.

Self-Study Pages Answer Key

Unit 1
become, believe, usual, discovered, give, prefer, broke, eager, ended, promoted

Unit 2
awesome, sponsorships, believe, agent, fortune, recognize, attention, embarrassing, spectators, matter

Unit 3
problem, home, grow, follow, lose, gain, exercise, plan, noises, idle, people, mechanic

Unit 4
cousin, family, guests, relatives, event, forgive, close, customers, close, small

Unit 5
personal, complex, minimum, similar, complete, general, tough, extreme, energy, procrastinate

Unit 6
background, experience, management, position, hope, representative, hired, hoping, perfect, honestly, attitude, accept

Unit 7
handsome, attractive, fashionable, shorter, comfortable, personality, click, sight, romantic, athletic, curves, independent

Unit 8
violent, abandoned, blood, influence, entertainment, hamburger, scientists, frustration, peaceful, meditating, obsession, absorbing

Unit 9
couple, appreciative, treat, sure, insisted, leans, seventeen, flirt, cute, hug, granddaughter, weird

Unit 10
covered, bleeding, untroubled, hurtling, furious, tumbling, streaming, sucked, slamming, dying, miraculously, tremendous

Unit 11
system, rules, strict, business, formal, polite, adjusting, learning, appearance, informal, members, respect

Unit 12
lifestyle, gradual, addicted, improve, level, relaxation, recognized, improved, kicked, control, break, energy

Unit 13
traveling, worried, advance, pulled, sold, cheated, stranded, arguing, pointing, terminal, tour, patient

Unit 14
bills, million, debt, financially, victim, estate, high, feeling, shipping, results

Unit 15
dealing, share, managing, passed, expected, mind, cheerful, hole, memories, celebrate, lose, person

■ Coursebooks

■ Skills Books

www.impactseries.com